KEEPING IN TUNE WITH GOD:
LISTENING HEARTS DISCERNMENT
FOR CLERGY

Keeping in

Morehouse Publishing
NEW YORK • HARRISBURG • DENVER

Suzanne G. Farnham and
Timothy H. Grayson

Tune with God

Listening Hearts
Discernment for Clergy

with a Foreword by the Rt. Rev. Eugene Taylor Sutton

Morehouse Publishing, 4775 Linglestown Road,
Harrisburg, PA 17112
Morehouse Publishing, 445 Fifth Avenue, New York, NY 10016
*Morehouse Publishing is an imprint of
Church Publishing Incorporated.*
www.churchpublishing.org

Cover design by Laurie Klein Westhafer

Library of Congress Cataloging-in-Publication Data

Farnham, Suzanne G.
    Keeping in tune with God : Listening Hearts discernment for
    clergy / Suzanne G. Farnham and Timothy H. Grayson.
      p. cm.
    Includes bibliographical references.
    ISBN 978-0-8192-2445-3 (pbk.) — ISBN 978-0-8192-2446-0
    (ebook) 1. Clergy—Religious life. 2. Listening—Religious
    aspects—Christianity. 3. Discernment (Christian theology)
    I. Grayson, Timothy H. II. Title.
    BV4011.6.F37 2011
    248.8'92—dc22

                                                  2010053631

Printed in the United States of America

Contents

About Listening Hearts Ministries

Founded in 1990, Listening Hearts Ministries holds a vision of the Body of Christ as a community of faith, eager for God's guidance, alert to signs of the Spirit, and alive with the prayer of deep listening. It provides a range of programs, publications, and services that teach people the practice of spiritual discernment through prayerful listening in support-ive communities.

Listening Hearts program offerings include:

• Retreats based on *Listening Hearts: Discerning Call in Community* for congregations, campus ministries, groups of spiritual seekers, and organi-zations within the church.

• Workshops based on *Grounded in God: Listening Hearts Discernment for Group Deliberations* for decision-making bodies, groups seeking spiritual conflict resolution, and groups wishing to develop a mission statement using spiritual discernment.

• Retreats and workshops based on *Keeping in Tune with God: Listening Hearts Discernment for Clergy,* designed especially for clergy groups.

• In-depth leaders' training programs that prepare participants to teach the practice of spiritual discernment to others.

Programs can be custom designed to meet the needs of a specific group.

In addition to the books mentioned above, Listening Hearts publications include the *Listening Hearts Manual of Discussion Leaders*, *Listening Hearts Retreat Designs*, the *Listening Hearts Songbook*, and a newsletter, *Explorations*, that explores and reflects on aspects of spiritual discernment.

The Listening Hearts website, www.listeninghearts.org, provides detailed information about Listening Hearts programs and publications. It also has a section called *Heartlinks*, which features interactive creative meditation exercises that provide format and guidelines for a wide selection of contemplative meditation activities.

Acknowledgments

I can do nothing by myself. . . —John 5:29 (JB)

Above all, we are grateful to the Right Reverend Eugene Taylor Sutton, Bishop of Maryland, who made time in his exacting schedule to write a generous and thoughtful foreword for this book. We are thankful for the contribution of John McIntyre, a copyeditor for the previous Listening Hearts books, who kindly provided us with his time and expertise in the early stages of manuscript preparation. Finally, we deeply appreciate our editor, the Reverend Stephanie Spellers, who championed the concept of this book and always supported our work with her warmth and intelligence.

We could say much more and still fall short. . . .
—Wisdom 43:27 (JB)

Foreword

In an age when too much is expected of clergy—from excellence in preaching and pastoral skills to being a first-rate administrator of complex organizations—— we need to be reminded that the first duty of parish clergy is to maintain a healthy spiritual life, and to lead others into a personal relationship with the triune God.[1] This holy calling to be a minister of the divine life is the same today as it was in the early Church period, when the Apostle Paul instructed his young assistant Timothy to "train yourself in godliness."[2]

What qualifies a person to be ordained into this work? Denominational guidelines and processes for ordination notwithstanding, at the core of ministry is a *passion* for God, a love affair with the One who is the source of all light and life. The minister is the one who, because of that intense love for God and the things of God, will lay down his or her own life for the sake of the gospel. Clergy use all of the resources of the faith to guide others into this passionate love relationship with the Beloved, so that the vision of God can be realized in people's lives and in the world.

Without that passion, there is no priesthood. Without the fire of Christ that burns inside, all you have left is a well-meaning religious functionary, an ecclesiastical employee, who has been trained to manage an institution whose survival hangs on the slender thread of holding up the historical memory of its founders. As the great jazz saxophonist and composer Charlie Parker once said, "If it ain't in your heart, it ain't in your horn."

In this superb publication, Suzanne Farnham and Tim Grayson offer spiritual guidance and practical resources for clergy to reconnect with their passion. They recognize that ordained ministers will be pulled in many different directions due to the demands of their vocations, yet they will gently guide the reader into healthy practices that will restore spiritual balance in the midst of his or her ministry. Their wisdom in discerning the presence and action of the Spirit in the lives of clergy is impressive. I highly recommend this volume to all who dare to trust God to touch them in a new and profound way.

The Rt. Rev. Eugene Taylor Sutton
Bishop, Episcopal Diocese of Maryland

KEEPING IN TUNE WITH GOD: LISTENING HEARTS DISCERNMENT FOR CLERGY

Introduction

For this reason I remind you to rekindle the gift of God that is within you. . . . —2 Timothy 1:6

Why did the apostle Paul speak these words to his faithful companion, Timothy? Had his young disciple's passion for ministry ceased to blaze? Did Timothy need a good stirring of the embers to get him back on the road again, preaching and exhorting all those who crossed his path to turn their lives over to Christ? On the other hand, was Paul simply telling his protégé that it would be important to continually refresh the gift he had received from God in order to minister to others with maximum effectiveness?

We might never know the answer to those questions, but we do know from Scripture that Timothy received the Holy Spirit through the laying on of Paul's hands, and we can imagine Timothy kneeling reverently before his mentor, feeling the rough hands of the tentmaker-turned-apostle pressing down hard on his head, as if to emphasize the heavy burden of ministry that he would assume.

Fast-forward two thousand years. In many traditional churches today, bishops ordain priests and deacons through a prayerful appeal to the Holy Spirit, after which they lay hands on the ordinand's head while continuing to pray intently. At the rehearsal before the ordination service, some bishops tell the ordinands that they are going to press down hard on their heads, so that the new ministers will stiffen their spines and remain kneeling, rather than buckling under the pressure.

Those words at the rehearsal are a forewarning that the vocation to which they have been called has an uncompromising edge to it, along with all the joys that come with serving Christ. Regardless of where ordained persons find a ministry—in a church, a school, or a hospital—they will face situations that will tax their energies and spiritual resources. Unfortunately, maintaining a life in which ordained responsibilities, family, and outside pursuits are fruitful and balanced does not get any easier with age and experience. Even seasoned clergy can find it difficult to avoid the fallout from the multifarious demands of a vocation that asks so much from its practitioners. The path of ministry that once appeared straightforward and inviting can rapidly sprout potholes and ambiguous signposts. It is easy to lose one's way over such terrain.

Keeping in Tune with God is written for clergy who are looking for a way back to the broad and inviting path on which they once embarked for all the right reasons. The book also should be of interest to all those who are concerned with clergy wellness and who might be the first to notice the warning signs of stress, depression, and other disturbing conditions in their minister. Included in this group are spouses, partners, friends, lay leaders in the church, spiritual directors, and counselors.

Nowadays, a GPS device enables the driver of a vehicle to navigate a route to a distant city with reasonable confidence. If for any reason the driver takes a wrong turn, the device helpfully calculates an alternative route. In a similar fashion, discernment is an invaluable instrument for clergy seeking to navigate around an obstacle in their vocation or personal lives that could lead them abruptly to a dead-end rather than a clearly lighted highway.

Originating from the Latin word *discernere*, meaning "to separate," "to distinguish," "to determine," or "to sort out," discernment in classical spirituality referred to the process of identifying what spirit was at work in a situation: the Spirit of God or some other spirit.[1] In essence, discernment involves a careful sifting of our exterior and interior experiences to determine their source. To the extent that we can listen reverently while clinging to nothing—neither thoughts, feelings, material possessions, nor personal relationships—we clear space for the Holy Spirit to flow freely. If we release ourselves to the creative movement of that flow without forcing it, we can be carried by sacred currents to see new horizons. Paradoxically, discernment is both a gift from God and a deliberate commitment on our part to hear, and then respond to, God's call on our life.[2]

> Discernment is more than saying prayers that ask God to guide us in rational consideration of matters. It is a mode of prayer that involves opening our entire selves to the working of the Holy Spirit. It bids us to let go of preconceived ideas so that we can be open to new possibilities with a readiness to view things from new perspectives. Discernment beckons us to be still and listen with the ear of our heart. It draws us into alignment with God.[3]

Drawing on the substantial distillation of knowledge and experience of Quaker and Ignatian discernment detailed in two earlier books, *Listening Hearts: Discerning Call in Community*, and *Grounded in God: Listening Hearts Discernment for Group Deliberations*,[4] this new text lays out the principles of Listening Hearts discernment clearly and concisely, equipping clergy with the tools they need to become spiritually refreshed and reoriented, reconnecting with the gift of God that resides deep within them.

The authors know the demands of ministry first-hand and have sought to marry the foundations of discernment with hands-on information designed to help clergy help themselves—through individual work and group exercises that promote collegiality and underscore the mysterious movement of the Spirit among those who come together in faith to cultivate the practice of discernment.

Using a small group of praying people to help with discernment broadens perspective, brings added insight, and multiplies the prayer power. Addressing the issue of listening for God's call in community, Parker Palmer writes, ". . . a true community of discernment can help us sift and winnow the many messages we get from inside and outside ourselves, separating the wheat from the chaff."[5]

The first part of *Keeping in Tune with God* sets forth the basic principles of spiritual discernment with a particular emphasis on issues that clergy encounter at various stages of their ministries. Then, the appendices provide clergy with practical suggestions for implementing the principles of spiritual discernment that were originally presented in *Listening Hearts* and *Grounded in God*. In common with those titles, this addition to the Listening Hearts library includes endnotes for each chapter, which further elucidate the text and guide the reader to more in-depth discussions of topics.

This book can serve as an introduction to spiritual discernment for clergy who may not necessarily be acquainted with the earlier Listening Hearts titles. At the same time, some familiarity with those books will be useful to ordained ministers who seek to draw closer to God by incorporating an array of proven spiritual practices into their increasingly fragmented lives.

For example, clergy may wish to consult *Listening Hearts* to develop more intimate relationships with God, their families, and their friends, and to navigate other pressing concerns in their personal lives. They may choose to work with *Grounded in God* in order to cultivate the practice of prayerful listening and consensus-building in their congregations, thus deepening the bonds of Christian community. Finally, clergy are invited to strengthen collegiality among their peers by forming support groups based on the principles put forth in both *Listening Hearts* and *Grounded in God.*

The authors hope that *Keeping in Tune with God* will be a valuable resource for all clergy who detect an uneasy dissonance in their vocations and long for the harmony that once underscored their relationship with God. These dedicated servant leaders can take heart in the knowledge that this harmony continues to echo deep within them, albeit faintly, and can once again resound strongly through their commitment to the practice of discernment and, above all, the boundless grace of God.

> *How could we sing the Lord's song in a foreign land?*
> *—Psalm 137:4*

ONE

The Demands of Ordained Ministry

When my spirit is faint within me, you are there to watch over my steps. In the path that I should take they have hidden a snare for me. —Psalm 142:3 (REB)

Hidden within every crisis is an invitation to grow wiser and closer to God. In this regard, clergy enjoy a special privilege. Difficult circumstances are built into their vocations. Fortunately, the discipline of spiritual discernment, drawn from core tenets of their faith, offers a way to traverse the rough terrain. Ordained ministers who journey arm-in-arm with God find themselves traveling their true paths. If they make it a priority to stay centered in God as they put one foot in front of the other, they will unselfconsciously lead others in the right direction. Immersion in God's presence brings guidance and solace, rejuvenating ministry on a day-to-day basis. But worldly forces consistently fight against this call to stillness before God.

Busyness

An ordained person is expected to be a pastor, preacher, teacher, theologian, administrator, spiritual leader, and role model—ever ready to respond to the desires and needs of both the congregation and the surrounding community. It is easy for clergy to get caught up in expectations projected upon them by their parishioners, finding themselves drawn into frantic activity to prove their value to their congregations—and perhaps to themselves.[1] They may busy themselves in work that reflects the imbalanced priorities of the world, forgetting that it is in returning and rest that they are saved, in quietness and in confidence that they find their strength.[2]

A hectic schedule can be a misplaced effort to earn respect and affection, which invariably leads to exhaustion and spiritual aridity.[3] Prayer gets squeezed in between meetings and appointments or dwindles altogether. A desire to serve God morphs into a flurry of activity that serves a hungry ego. The result is burnout.

With luck, clergy may be saved from burnout by church members, friends, or family members who understand the demands of ministry and who may have witnessed other clergy implosions in the past. Through a combination of grace and sudden insight, perhaps with outside help, some clergy rescue themselves from the precipice of mind-numbing fatigue, addressing the workaholism that tends to take over their lives.

AUTHORITY

Ordination designates clergy as spiritual leaders. They preside at the Lord's Supper. They proclaim the word of God from the pulpit, interpreting Scripture for the present time and place. Certain orders of clergy are authorized to absolve people of their sins. Members of a congregation may defer to them when facing important decisions. Some people idealize them; others treat them as idols. All of this presents the ordained minister with a temptation to feel self-important,[4] revel in special treatment, or make use of an elevated position for personal benefit. Therefore, clergy must constantly strive to maintain a God-centered perspective.

Because of the lofty status sometimes accorded them, ordained ministers are likely to carry a special burden, as well. People have unrealistic expectations of them and fail to appreciate their human limitations.[5] While clergy may get undeserved credit for things that go well, they are sure to get unwarranted blame for things that go wrong. They are likely to be inappropriate targets of frustration and stored-up anger that hover beneath the surface in people they serve. Ironically, attempts by some people to attack or even demonize an ordained minister can reinforce his or her sense of importance. In some cases, it tempts targeted clergy to view themselves as martyrs or prophets, charged with defending the faith in a hostile environment. Of course, God does call many people, including ordained ministers, to prophetic ministries. Nevertheless, it is possible for clergy who are fixated on their own agendas to fancy themselves as prophets instead of focusing their attention on God's purpose for them. If spiritual leaders are to travel a steady path through the complexities of ministry, they must diligently cultivate discerning hearts and minds.

Clergy generally score high marks on psychological instruments that rate interpersonal skills and elicit evidence of a strong desire to help others. Unfortunately, the same predisposition to servant ministry can mask a need for control and a craving for admiration and attention.[6]

MONEY

Financial pressures are an ever-present reality in the lives of most ordained ministers. Monetary considerations pose perplexing concerns for clergy. Ministers frequently complete seminary with considerable debt. Salaries for church work tend to be modest. A call to an affluent parish may be easier to hear than a call to urban or rural ministry where problems can be big and the pay small. A desire to provide well for one's family can dim the view of one's true calling. Pressure from family members can reinforce the dilemma. Most clergy understand that the call to minister in Christ's name embraces a willingness to forego many material comforts enjoyed by their peers. Nevertheless, the trappings of secular success can prove alluring.

Beyond that, financial concerns inevitably surface in any congregation or church organization. Establishing budgetary priorities is no easy matter. Each aspect of church life competes with others for funding: salaries and benefits for clergy, compensation packages for lay employees, music expenditures, Christian education, buildings and grounds, outreach, youth ministry, liturgy and worship. Raising money and allocating resources involve questions of justice, integrity, respect for divergent points of view, and the centrality of God. Do we give to a budget or do we give to God? Does our mission dictate the budget, or does the budget dictate our mission? A true story speaks to the issue: Members of a congregation were reluctant to increase expenditures for outreach because it seemed there were no funds to cover it. The pastor suggested developing the numbers for the budget based on what the church would ideally be doing and then work out where the money would come from. Taking a big leap, the congregation increased the outreach budget substantially. Soon, contributions to the church began to rise dramatically. This began an upward spiral that sees both outreach to people in need and parish income continue to grow as the years go by. Decisions about money are a theological and spiritual issue.

These various difficulties are in no way exclusive to clergy, but they can pour down upon ordained ministers with particular force. These perplexities defy easy solutions. But, as spiritual leaders, clergy must set their courses in alignment with God if they are to remain true to their vocations.

Spiritual discernment does not produce a roadmap. Rather, it helps the traveler notice the signs that God provides, to interpret them, and finally, to follow them. When we engage in spiritual discernment, God does not tell us precisely what to do, but God does point the direction and guide us forward. Through the practice of spiritual discernment, we walk close to God, the source of all comfort and wisdom. When we travel with God, all things work together for good.[7]

Set your mind on God's kingdom and his justice before everything else, and all the rest will come to you, as well.
—Matthew 6:33 (REB)

TWO

Opening Ourselves to God

O God, you are my God, eagerly I seek you, my soul thirsts for you, my flesh faints for you, as in a barren land where there is no water. —Psalm 63:1

Those who wish to walk with God must detach themselves from long-held habits of thought and action that separate them from the divine presence. The allure of power and popularity, feverish activity, and myriad temptations that skim across the surface of life prevent many people from taking on the arduous task of finding their true selves.[1] Digging through the layers that prop up the false self is hazardous work because these layers form the strata upon which people construct a fragile sense of control over their lives.[2] Those who persist in this task of spiritual excavation eventually experience the collapse of the false self as the ground beneath them shifts. As their former foundations crumble, their illusory sense of control falls away. Having reached truly firm terrain, they find themselves face to face with the reality of God, whose presence provides enduring stability.

Opening ourselves to God requires submission and surrender to the divine will. In some cases, this assent to God's indwelling comes only after a hotly contested struggle in which God is the victor.[3] Although such epic contests are not uncommon in the spiritual realm, more often our openness to God comes after a lengthy sojourn in the wilderness,[4] as we realize that we have wandered far from the source that once nourished us and assuaged our thirst. We become aware of the layers of detritus that cover up the truth within us, which we need to strip away in order to find our freedom in God.

Because God dwells at the very center of our being, when we open our hearts to God we discover the dictates of our true selves. Gradually, the true self grows stronger while the false self dissipates. We find ourselves becoming the people God created us to be, ready to inhabit our inner core, where God's love illuminates and nurtures a trusting spirit.

We are willing to seek discernment in earnest only if we believe that God loves us more than we love ourselves and wants only the very best for us. Otherwise, we want what we want and hesitate to take the chance that God might ask something different of us. Understandably, we are reluctant to relinquish control. However, if we believe that God's love exceeds all that we can desire and pray for,[5] and that in God all things work together for good, then we trust that if we train our ears to hear God's word for us, we are in fact pursuing what is best for us. We must fling the doors of our soul wide open to God if we are to enter wholeheartedly into spiritual discernment.

If the Spirit of God is to flow freely through us, we must keep those doors to our innermost selves open, and clear the space within.[6] One discipline for establishing and maintaining this commitment is contemplative prayer.[7] When engaged in contemplation,[8] one enters a state of stillness,[9] ignoring all thoughts and feelings, neither clinging to them nor fighting them, simply paying no attention to them, letting them come and letting them go. Thoughts and feelings will float by like shadows at the periphery, but are not to become vivid and occupy the space reserved for God.[10] Over time, this inner sanctuary will grow stronger, expand, and eventually may penetrate the entire person, issuing forth as unceasing prayer of the heart.[11]

A prayer called the Jesus Prayer developed and flourished in the Orthodox tradition. In its simplest form, the words "Lord Jesus Christ, have mercy on me"[12] are repeated over and over, day and night—whether walking, sitting, or lying down—until they take on a life of their own.[13] Eventually, the words begin to say themselves subliminally within the heart, ready to surface as needed.[14] This prayer continues to draw men and women in both the East and West into lives of unceasing prayer, keeping them in tune with God, even when they are engaged in the normal activities of daily life.[15]

More recently, a cluster of American Trappist monks have led a movement teaching centering prayer.[16] This practice requires commitment to sitting in contemplative stillness at an appointed time at least once each day, usually for about twenty minutes. Each person adopts a sacred word of one or two syllables to silently utter as an aid to becoming centered and empty when thoughts or feelings begin to move to center stage. Examples of sacred words adopted by people include God, Jesus, Spirit, Abba, peace, love, and trust. In and of itself, the meaning of the word is not important. The intent of the word is to assent to God's presence deep within. The sacred word is a vehicle which, when uttered silently, carries the person back toward the center. Centering prayer has brought many seekers into more intimate relationship with God.

When we open ourselves to God's presence and abandon ourselves to divine truth, the creative power of God's love stirs within us.[17] We begin to see things that we never saw before. God starts to do things through us that surpass what we could ever do of our own accord. New life springs forth from our depths.

I know your works. Look, I have set before you an open door, which no one is able to shut. —Revelation 3:8

THREE

The Paradox of Humility

What does the Lord require of you but to do justice, and to love kindness, and to walk humbly with your God?
—Micah 6:8

As we walk arm-in-arm with God, day in and day out, we gradually develop a sense of God's boundless wisdom and goodness as well as the tremendous power of God's love and truth. As we become immersed in the divine presence, we come to perceive God's greatness, which in turn reveals our own smallness. It becomes clear that our view of reality is minuscule compared with God's.[1] Motives, desires, fears, and forces that are hidden from us affect our behavior and the events that unfold around us. We see that our perception of people, situations, events, and issues is limited by time, geography, culture, and personality type. God alone sees all things from every possible perspective—past, present, and future.

The closer a person's relationship with God, the more that person becomes cloaked in humility.[2] Because humble people are God-centered and know that all that is good in them comes from God, they can receive praise and compliments graciously and unselfconsciously, perhaps with a grateful smile or a quiet "thank you."[3] They are able to dispassionately assess their strengths without lapsing into self-glorification. Similarly, as they come to realize that every human being is fallible, they can accept their own weaknesses without falling prey to self-debasement[4] and, at the same time, become less inclined to judge others.[5] They find themselves able to accept criticism without becoming defensive and willingly submit to the Holy Spirit as they consider critical comments. Humble people are neither strident nor servile, but speak and act with serene confidence that God's purpose is being served.

When life is firmly anchored in God, it becomes secure, and feelings of inadequacy can dissolve. One woman who had felt the weight of a heavy inferiority complex for many years knew rationally that she was not inferior; logic did not support it. But no matter how hard she tried or how much she prayed, she could not stop feeling inferior. Then, as her relationship with God grew more and more intimate, suddenly—without warning—she woke up one morning and her inferiority complex had vanished forever. It was not self-confidence, but confidence in

God that had broken through. It was an unanticipated transformation.

Clarity about our own limitations does not make
us timid. Embodying the humility that is the mark
of Jesus does not impede our engagement with the
world. Instead, humility propels us into mission,
emboldened by trust in Christ, who came not to
lord it over others but to serve.[6] Once we have done
our utmost to discern what God would have us do,
we know that we must act on that understanding.
At the same time, we realize that it is imperative to
continue discerning what God is asking of us, secure
in the knowledge that if we did not get it right, the
Holy Spirit will correct our course. If we faithfully
follow the discernment that comes to us and stay in
tune with God, we can be confident that God will
make good use of what we do. We can trust that
even when we get it wrong, God will make us wiser
for it.

Humility is a profoundly mysterious quality.[7] It cannot
be attained by seeking it. It cannot be achieved by
striving for it. Humility emerges only after a drastic
reordering of priorities in which God's transcendence
is reflected in a quieting of human endeavor.[8] Then
we begin to view life through a different lens, perceiv-
ing the action of the Holy Spirit in even the most
mundane transactions. For those who steadfastly
journey with God, the veil of reality may at times
fall back to reveal the glory that underlies all things.[9]

Filled with awe at God's magnificence, feelings of superiority and certitude disappear, clearing space for divine truth and love to expand.[10] Thus, humility wells up from within those who dwell in God's presence.

> *"All who exalt themselves will be humbled, and all who humble themselves will be exalted."*
> *—Matthew 23:12*

F O U R

The Paradox of Detachment

For God alone my soul waits in silence. —*Psalm 62:1*

Humility is one side of a valuable coin. The other side of the coin is detachment—a disengagement from things both tangible and intangible so as to view and experience life from a broader, more comprehensive perspective.[1] Holding on to what is good (a form of attachment) holds us back from finding what is better.[2] Thus, detachment frees us to move continually toward a higher good. Humility is a natural outgrowth of detachment. Similarly, detachment is a natural outgrowth of humility. The two are bound together in unity of purpose.[3]

While humility cannot be attained through conscious effort, detachment reflects a deliberate choice to navigate through life aware that attraction to ideas, things, and people can both liberate and ensnare. A compelling new idea may prompt us to test its appeal to others and advocate its acceptance over competing ideas. However, if our fervor for an idea stirs in us a compulsion to see it accepted by others, or if we believe that our idea is superior without question, we allow desire and pride to infect an enthusiasm that initially was pure and dispassionate.[4]

Detachment necessitates that we keep an ever-watchful eye on our emotions, because our zeal for an idea, material goods, a person, or even our concept of God[5] can spawn a rigidity that insists on having its own way. Any circumstance in which we insist that there is no viable alternative to the path we have set for ourselves, and perhaps for others as well, should set off alarm bells in our head. We have achieved detachment when we are able to step back and view ourselves objectively, alert to any attempt on our own part to force acceptance of anything that we hold dear.

One of the basic principles of spiritual discernment is to hold desires and opinions—and even our convictions—lightly. This fundamental tenet reflects teachings on detachment in all of the major contemplative traditions.[6] It does not mean that we should not have strong values or deep convictions. It does mean that if we cling tightly to those values and convictions, they take center stage, shutting God out and impeding our own spiritual growth. It also means that those who disagree with us are likely to feel pressure that can cause them to resist our point of view.[7]

Convictions, by definition, reflect firmly held values and beliefs. If they are of God, it is safe for us to hold them lightly—resting upon open hands—because no one can take them away from us.[8] If we hold onto them with clenched fists close to our chest, we create a barrier that keeps God out. Perhaps the conviction needs strengthening or modification. If our hands are gently open, the Holy Spirit can reshape and mature our understanding, or shed light on any error if that is what is needed. Convictions that are held too tightly become calcified.[9] Convictions that are open to the light of God's love and truth grow ever stronger and healthier.

From a practical point of view, convictions held lightly are more accessible to those who oppose them. Convictions held in a tight clasp are hard for others to see. If we clench something, we are tense and give off negative energy. Those who disagree with us are likely to become defensive, perhaps combative. However, if we serenely hold our convictions in open hands, they are in plain view, and people who do not like them may feel safe in looking at them from a distance. Possibly, those with opposing views may slowly move closer. In time, they might even feel safe enough to touch them, possibly be willing to try them on.

For many clergy in positions of leadership,[10] to be detached seems inconsistent with their vocations. They see it as their responsibility to put forth a clear vision, take strong positions, and stand firm. Effective leaders are indeed people of vision who are willing to take stands on issues and able to articulate them with clarity. But strong leaders who are detached have no need to be unyielding or manipulative. Detachment calls forth leadership that cultivates a trinity of trust: (1) confidence that God cares deeply, is the source of all wisdom, and is always working to bring about unity and wholeness; (2) confidence that the ordained leader is a person of integrity committed to a close personal relationship with God; and (3) confidence that the leader is tuned in to the people, appreciates the value of their thoughts and feelings, and is helping them grow into a more intimate relationship with God. Such leaders listen and grow with their flock, paving the way for the shared ministry of all baptized Christians.

Spiritual discernment proceeds from a desire to detect the currents of God's love and truth and be carried by the Spirit toward the very heart of God. Trusting God enough to pursue detachment transmits a serenity that is a deep well for spiritual discernment.[11]

> *For with you is the fountain of life;*
> *and in your light we see light.*
> —Psalm 36:9

FIVE

Engaging the Rational Faculties

*An intelligent mind acquires knowledge, and the ear of the
wise seeks knowledge. —Proverbs 18:15*

"Let your mind descend into your heart," say Eastern
Orthodox mystics.[1] Their words hold valuable
wisdom for spiritual discernment. They do not suggest
that we discard our minds, nor do they ask us to
ignore our intellects. Rather they speak of letting our
mental faculties become integrated into the very core
of who we are.

Mature spiritual discernment begins with vigorous
mental activity. The first order of business is to clarify
the discernment issue under consideration, working
to refine the wording until the question comes into
sharp focus. Addressing the question directly to God
can place God at the center of our quest.[2] By steering
away from either/or questions or those that ask for a
"yes" or "no" response, we can avoid limiting God's
options.[3] Then, if we prime our hearts and minds to
open wide, the Spirit may stream in to carry us to an

entirely new place where we see possibilities beyond anything we could discover on our own.[4]

After the question becomes clear, concise, and inviting, it is time to gather information and ideas. By reading relevant material, seeking counsel from people we respect, evaluating data, identifying ways to handle the situation, listing pros and cons, and weighing options, we can develop a preliminary position. If we can hold our intellectual work lightly when it is completed and not cling to it, it can simply float at the periphery while our minds descend into our hearts. Then, if we gently rest in God, thoughts and feelings that emanate from the issue can bathe in the divine presence. Remaining still for an extended period allows God's Spirit to flow freely within us.

Once a person assimilates the sequence to follow, the process can become fluid and take its own course. For example, a pastor of an urban church pondered how to engage her congregation more fully in hands-on ministry in the neighborhood. Alcoholics Anonymous and other twelve-step groups held weekly meetings in the church hall but, understandably, did not wish to align themselves with any particular faith. Nevertheless, the pastor continued to talk with group members, convinced that the Spirit was moving in a direction that might prove fruitful. One day, the house manager of a nearby group home for recovering addicts called to ask if the church could help a resident pay his rent. After a few minutes, the pastor realized that the house manager was a member of the Narcotics Anonymous group that met at her church but had never noticed the name of the church outside the entrance. As they established the connection between themselves, they began to explore how the church and the group home might enter into a ministry partnership. The pastor and a man from her congregation began visiting the group home to conduct a weekly Bible study, making it clear to the residents that they were not recruiting new parishioners but exploring the mysterious movement of God in their lives. In return, residents of the home began to help with maintenance of the church building and grounds, and some of them began attending the church. The ministry partnership continues to evolve. An idea that had floated at the periphery of the pastor's mind for several months, untrammeled by anxiety about initiating a new ministry, had blossomed into reality.

Jesus counsels us to be wise as serpents and innocent as doves.[5] These are good words to remember for spiritual discernment. If we do our research, think things through, apply the best of our human capabilities, and let ourselves be neither ignorant nor naïve, we are ready to remind ourselves that actual wisdom comes from God. By putting ourselves in God's hands, we allow the Spirit of love and truth to bring a new dimension to our consciousness. This is not likely to negate our human insights, but may very well radically alter our comprehension of a situation and its possibilities.

Our willingness to allow God to work in us in God's time, rather than anxiously imposing our own deadline on the process, will be rewarded. Over time, the simple act of faithfully putting ourselves before God and seeking God's counsel may help shape and refine our question. The more we come to God in true humility, the more room the Spirit will have to give form to the thoughts and desires that whirl inside us, seeking articulation.[6]

Ultimately, spiritual discernment challenges us to trust the profound wisdom, goodness, and faithfulness of God. On occasion, the direction that seemed clear to us during prayer one morning may be shrouded in mist the next day, leading us to question not only our own judgment but also the guidance of God that we are diligently seeking. At times, we will misread signs. Inevitably, we will make mistakes. Yet, if we continue moving forward in an intimate relationship with God, keeping our inner ears and eyes alert, God will guide us, defend us, and comfort us without ceasing. Spiritual discernment is an ever-evolving journey into God. It always sheds enough light to help us see the next step as we seek to follow our true path.

For the Lord gives wisdom; from his mouth
come knowledge and understanding.
—Proverbs 2:6

SIX

Drawing upon Creativity
and Imagination

*Then the angel showed me the river of life . . . flowing
crystal clear down the middle of the city street.*
—Revelation 22:1–2 (JB)

Scientific knowledge, intellectual inquiry, and sound
reasoning are important to staying in tune with God,
but by themselves, they can neither reveal ultimate
reality nor bring wholeness to our lives. Developing
into the people God created us to be requires a mysterious journey that defies logic. It involves exploring
questions that have no definitive answers—questions
related to love, truth, forgiveness, power, authority,
suffering, death, and new life.

One way to chart our true paths and make choices
consistent with them is to open ourselves to dynamic
artistic expression. When we desire God's guidance
in a given situation—after we clearly and explicitly
identify our issue for discernment, think it through
carefully, and consider options—we are ready to feel

the situation deeply. Then, to prepare appropriate space, we can offer it all to God and let go of related thoughts and feelings so they hover in suspension at the periphery. Once firmly planted in God's presence, we are primed to receive any imaginative flash that might spring forth from deep within.

We can invite such a creative burst by identifying an area of personal interest that might contain a symbol that could inform the issue: such as a scene from nature; a person, image, or excerpt from Scripture; a segment from a play, movie, or novel; a type of animal; a piece of music; a particular kind of dance; or an analogy from family life or the business world. Not every issue will lend itself to the same type of imaginative association.[1] There are times when a Bible passage will seem like a natural choice; another time, music might most effectively unlock what lies hidden beneath the surface. Once an area of interest has been identified, it is time to let the mind rest while remaining centered in God. In no way try to force or manufacture a symbol. Just stay immersed in God's presence as you hold your concern close to your heart. If in time something springs suddenly and spontaneously from the depths, hold it in reverence for a period of time. Then meditate on it, explore the implications of its every aspect, follow where it leads, and observe accompanying feelings.[2] Finally, become still again so that God can reshape your thoughts and craft you anew.

In spiritual discernment, vivid insight and clarity most often come through imaginative breakthroughs, either visual or auditory.[3] As an example, in one discernment group session, at various times the seeker of discernment mentioned coming up against a wall. One member of the group observed this and asked what the wall was made of. The seeker quietly considered the question. Then suddenly a startled look swept across her face and she blurted out, "Jell-O." Through several follow-up questions, it became clear that the wall was not impassable and in fact could quite easily be penetrated.[4] From that point on, things fell easily into place.[5]

Symbols that bubble to the surface from deep within have the power to carry us to new places that can broaden our perspective, refine our concept of truth, deepen our compassion, and draw us into more intimate relationships with God and other people. God's creative energy is alive at all times in all places, ever ready for us to tap into so that it can flow freely into every molecule of our being.

All my springs are in you. —Psalm 87:7

SEVEN

Coming Together in the Spirit

And now with all our heart we follow you; we fear you and seek your presence. —The Prayer of Azariah, v. 18

As appointed leaders in communities of faith, ordained ministers are in a unique position to transmit the practice of spiritual discernment to those they serve by the way they conduct business at staff meetings, committee and board meetings, and gatherings for deliberations that involve the entire community. When clergy engage congregations and other groupings experientially in centered listening and consensus building, they develop and strengthen the discipline of discernment within themselves while cultivating discerning communities. Over time their ministry becomes increasingly God-centered and collaborative.

Any group inspired to work in greater harmony with God—be it a governing board, a committee, or a support group—can do so by adopting five important practices:

- Always gather with a commitment to seeking God's guidance.

- Enter into silence.

- Take time to become immersed in the divine presence.

- Listen to one another with empathy and respect.

- Connect with God at the center of all present, especially those with differing views.

These elements combine to slowly give rise to a spiritual consensus that unifies the group and puts it in sync with God. This does not connote uniformity. Opinions will likely vary. Unity emerges when everyone has been given adequate opportunity to express their thoughts and feelings; everyone feels listened to, loved, and respected; and the group has found a way forward that all can accept.[1] By seeking to dwell at God's center where all things are in right relationship, members of the group become one.

The discipline of spiritual discernment brings forth spiritual consensus.[2] Consensus literally means sensing together. Generic consensus involves arriving at a sense of the group through study, discussion, and possibly debate, without taking a vote or polling the group. It requires finding common ground. Spiritual consensus is a very specific type of consensus that, in addition, requires being attuned to the Holy Spirit in, through, with, and among those present. It is marked by signs of the Spirit—signs such as convergence; persistence; joy; energy; tears of release; sudden, unanticipated awareness or insight; and a shared sense of God's peace.[3] The stronger and more numerous the signs, the stronger the consensus. The one sign that is essential is God's peace. For that reason, it is of utmost importance that any person who is experiencing its opposite (a feeling of agitation) speak up, because this is an indication that more prayer and more exploration are needed. It signals that something is out of kilter somewhere or with someone.

To illustrate this point: A deliberative body was working on an important matter. One member felt churned up by the group's decision but thought these unsettled feelings might be telling him that he was feeling threatened by the impending action, and perhaps his uneasiness said more about him than about the situation. As things played out, the decision led to a disaster. When the man subsequently told the group about the concerns with which he had wrestled, it turned out that another person had experienced similar reservations and had refrained from saying anything for similar reasons. Had they spoken up, the group could have helped them discover the source of their feelings, and the calamity likely would have been avoided. In spiritual discernment, we need to be as open and honest as possible, trusting that the Spirit of love and truth in the community will make all well.

However, even if we do everything right as we pursue spiritual consensus, our choices may lead to what appear to be mistakes. Sometimes there are lessons that we must learn in order to grow in the wisdom needed to live out our calls effectively. Often experiential learning by trial and error is the only path to authentic knowledge.[4] From that perspective, what seems to be a mistake may not actually be one. And this much is certain: If we try our very best to follow the way of spiritual discernment, we will be staying close to God, and all that we do will be used constructively by the creator of all that is.

Clergy who commit themselves to lives of discernment tend to unselfconsciously draw members of their communities into more intimate, more mature relationships with both God and one another. Deep compassion creates a safe environment in which people can dare to be open and honest about all that they think and feel. When members of a group are able to explore their inmost thoughts, including their instincts, without guise, the atmosphere is right for God's truth to emerge. As a community of faith comes to serve as a channel of God's compassion for every member, God's reconciling love is incarnated. It is then that the Body of Christ comes fully to life in that time and place.

If you continue in my word . . . you will know
the truth . . . —John 9:31–32

EIGHT

Forging Deep Collegiality

*How good and pleasant it is when God's people live
together in unity! —Psalm 133:1 (TNIV)*

The path to deep collegiality among ordained ministers begins when clergy recognize that they share a
common mission. It opens up as they develop watch-
ful eyes that observe the Spirit working in each other.
It continues to open before them if a gentle atmosphere of compassion and respect makes it safe for
them to share the thoughts of their hearts, no matter
what those thoughts may be. The path widens as the
ministers involved see how individual gifts serve the
whole body, as they come to see more clearly the
importance of both unity and diversity in the Body of
Christ. As the Spirit speaks the truth in love through
its members, the group finds solid ground for true
fellowship.

Many active clergy participate in some kind of
colleague group that provides opportunities to share
problems, seek input from others, and find comfort

in times of difficulty. Group members get good ideas from each other and gain assurance that they are not alone. Yet in-depth encounters with one another and powerful experiences of God are not always forthcoming.

Often, ordained ministers desire to be part of a group that they can truly experience as the Body of Christ, in which they can share their spiritual struggles in confidence. They want to connect with Christ in their colleagues on a regular basis. But the ways of secular culture are deeply embedded in our behavior, and it takes determination and persistence to shed them. Fear can hold us back from exposing our doubts, incompetence, and especially our stupidity. It is hard to embrace the model of the wounded healer—we are reluctant to let people see us as we really are. We also may be afraid to find out what God really wants from us. And the numinous can be frightening.

Yet when a clergy support group provides an atmosphere conducive to powerful encounters with Christ, members find the effectiveness of their ministries strengthened and their lives enriched. They come to know at their core that God hears the cries of the broken-hearted, that God's yearning is for reconciliation and healing that make us whole.

Spiritual discernment[1] fosters deep collegiality through profound prayerful listening and creative engagement with Scripture. It draws upon the imagination to bring forth expression of God's action in one's life, which may have gone unnoticed, not been taken seriously, or never been carried forward. It evokes signs of the Spirit that give evidence of God's presence. By eliciting consciousness of how God is acting in one person or situation, it spurs all involved to look at their own lives to see where God is at work. It impels them to share their own spiritual experience. It reveals that all who dare trust in God are touched by the sun—and that exposure is full of grace. God is present in the world. We all know this at some level, but spiritual discernment lets us know it in our bones. With spiritual discernment at the heart of a colleague group, clergy can be continually reenergized, renewed, and refreshed.

*Let each of you look not to your own interests,
but to the interests of others. Let the same mind be in
you that was in Christ Jesus. —Philippians 2:4–5*

NINE

The Springs of Spiritual Refreshment

. . . And the parched ground shall become a pool, and the thirsty land springs of water . . . —Isaiah 35:7 (KJV)

The elements of spiritual discernment are internal, inaudible and invisible. As they coalesce over time, they gather strength to nourish the forces of wholeness in the visible, tangible world. Each element makes an essential contribution:

- **Silence** creates space for us to get in touch with God at our center.

- **Centering in God** connects us with the source of love and truth.

- As love and truth find a home in us, **humility** begins to move in, which helps us recognize our need for other people, expose the thoughts of our hearts to them, respect what they have to say, and be willing to learn from them.

- Humility invites **detachment**, which enables us to become non-combative. The more we create an atmosphere that is non-aggressive, the safer it is for us to let down our defenses.

- Stripping away our defenses frees us to fully engage our **thoughts, feelings, senses, intuition, and imagination,** thus opening the way to wholeness.

When these elements move together, they carve out channels of honesty and compassion that allow sacred inner currents[1] to break through to the surface.

Spiritual discernment entails recurring patterns of withdrawal and return.[2] By immersing ourselves in the interior world, we slowly discover the ground of our being. As the waters of the Spirit within us converge, they turn into springs that release the life-giving power of God into the world, to refresh and renew all creation.

You cut openings for springs and torrents; you dried up ever-flowing streams … —Psalm 74:15

APPENDICES OF PRACTICAL SUGGESTIONS

Introduction

The nine chapters of this book explore basic principles of spiritual discernment, particularly as they apply to ordained ministers. These Appendices of Practical Suggestions lay out step-by-step ways for clergy and church leaders to integrate this practice of discernment into their lives and ministries, making use of two companion books, *Listening Hearts: Discerning Call in Community* by Farnham, Gill, McLean, and Ward, and *Grounded in God: Listening Hearts Discernment for Group Deliberations* by Farnham, Hull, and McLean.

Unfortunately, it is all too easy for busy clergy to become isolated from their congregations, as much as they might want to stay in tune with their members and God, for whom they have sacrificed so much to serve. The press of administrative duties, pastoral responsibilities, and the deadline for a Sunday sermon that seems to circle round more quickly each week all contribute to a hive of activity that allows little time for rest and reflection. Little by little, pastors can become consumed by the constant need to "do" rather than "be," while opportunities to listen deeply to a person in need of counsel or a friendly chat grow increasingly rare.

As time to listen to others decreases, the ability to be present to people dissipates. Meanwhile, an alienation that seemingly comes from nowhere may slowly creep in to edge out what was once a quiet empathy. On a larger scale, an inability to listen to another person may easily be transmitted to the congregation as a whole, with potentially disastrous consequences. The people in the pews may believe their pastor has lost touch with them, and the pastor may feel that the people are shutting him out. In cases like these, and even in congregations where communications are good, it helps to have an instrument that will facilitate listening among all members of a faith community. This can also help them hear God's call on their lives with more clarity. For this reason, the authors especially hope that Appendix 1, "Developing a Congregation that Listens to God and One Another," will be a useful resource for pastors, who are directed to *Grounded in God* for more detailed information.

Each appendix outlines a workable way to move toward a specific goal. This does not mean that there is no other way to approach that objective. The purpose is to provide the reader with field-tested models from which to work. The guidelines can be adapted to accommodate the particular needs of a given person, group, or community.

Those who cultivate discerning communities mysteriously find themselves keeping in tune with God. If you have questions or concerns as you work with the ideas in these appendices, feel free to contact Listening Hearts Ministries at listening@verizon.net or through the website, www.listeninghearts.org.

Appendix 1
Developing a Congregation that Listens to God and One Another

Deep, prayerful listening is the bedrock of spiritual discernment. The Discernment Listening Guidelines, listed below and detailed in Appendix 1 of *Grounded in God*, can change the culture of an entire congregation or ministry if implemented with careful education and conscientious follow-up procedures:

DISCERNMENT LISTENING GUIDELINES

1. Take time to become settled in God's presence.

2. Listen to others with your entire self (senses, feelings, intuition, imagination, and rational faculties).

3. Do not interrupt.

4. Pause between speakers to absorb what has been said.

5. Do not formulate what you want to say while someone else is speaking.

6. Speak for yourself only, expressing your own thoughts and feelings, referring to your own experiences. Avoid being hypothetical. Steer away from broad generalizations.

7. Do not challenge what others say.

8. Listen to the group as a whole—to those who have not spoken aloud as well as to those who have.

9. Generally, leave space for anyone who may want to speak a first time before speaking a second time yourself.

10. Hold your desires and opinions—even your convictions—lightly.

To effectively implement the above guidelines:

1. Begin by introducing them to the leadership of the congregation as follows:

- Assemble the group in a circle.

- Distribute copies of the guidelines to each member of the group. Attractive laminated copies can be purchased from Listening Hearts Ministries (www.listeninghearts.org).

- Going around the circle, each person in turn reads one guideline aloud. Pause between readers to give everyone time to assimilate the guideline as well as raise questions or concerns, and offer comments. Emphasize that it is important for people to speak up if they do not understand a guideline or do not agree with it. The objective is to develop a common under-standing of the intent and value of each guideline. This usually takes about forty-five minutes, sometimes slightly less, occasionally much longer. It can be scheduled for a single meeting or can be spread over a number of consecutive meetings.

- After all of the guidelines have been processed, ask the group if it is willing to adopt them as group norms. If some members are reluctant, ask if they would be agreeable to using them for a specified period on a trial basis.

2. It is essential that everyone understand that each person has both the privilege and the responsibility of helping the group stay faithful to the guidelines. The convener of the meeting cannot effectively police the listening habits of the group. If everyone shares responsibility for the guidelines, working collaboratively in a way that is gentle, caring, and ever-vigilant, members will mature together as a listening community.

3. Once the group has agreed to use the guidelines at its meetings, it is important that participants read them aloud at the beginning of each meeting (each guideline read by a different person, with a pause between readers). Then, at the end of each meeting, build in a few minutes for members to consider how well they did at abiding by them.

4. Once the guidelines have been introduced to the leadership, introduce them in the same way to all of the groups that are part of the congregation.

5. After all of the groups are acquainted with the guidelines, introduce them to the congregation as a whole at Sunday services, in the church's newsletter, in other printed materials, and on the church's website. The senior minister may want to reinforce the importance of the guidelines by discussing them in a letter sent to all members. Posters of the guidelines can be displayed in appropriate places. A supply of laminated copies to use at meetings can be kept in convenient places.

Appendix 2
Ways to Enter the Flow of the Spirit through Artistic Expression

Through a disciplined prayer life, marked by humility before God and detached from the material, spiritual, and psychological sirens that distract and ensnare, ordained ministers can stay in tune with God. The Holy Spirit moving within them may manifest itself in new and unexpected forms, expressing itself in ways that are both surprising and liberating. Men and women who once felt no personal attraction to the worlds of literature, art, drama, and music may discover an unexpected channel within themselves that can enliven their relationship with God in innovative and dynamic ways.

When artistic expression springs forth from contemplative prayer, it almost always taps into the currents of God's Holy Spirit. As we meditate on symbols that emerge from our time of prayer, we get in touch with deeper truths and unearth realities hitherto hidden from us. On occasion, profound transformation may occur. Simple procedures can provide a structure that invites the Spirit to flow freely, stimulates artistic expression, and brings forth God's guidance for our lives.

Well ahead of time, assemble artistic materials that you may need for your time of meditation.

1. Let yourself become still. Try to let your muscles relax. Let your thoughts and feelings come to rest. Let God's presence seep into your being. If you are unaccustomed to silence, begin by trying it for two minutes. Over time, gradually increase the time to five minutes and eventually to ten minutes.

2. Continue the silence, holding the current state of your life at the center of your being for a few minutes. If any specific issue or relationship is troubling you, let it emerge and come into focus. Carry this with you in your heart as you move into the Scripture.

3. Leaf through a Bible, looking for a passage, theme, image, or character that may speak to your situation. Perhaps read it in context, looking to see what precedes and follows it. Possibly locate parallel readings that tell the same story in different words or that have similar themes. If no Bible is available or if it is difficult to find a suitable passage, select one from the list at the end of these instructions.

4. Once the words permeate you, fall still and let your life situation and the Scripture simply envelop you.

5. Remain still until you feel moved to express yourself.

6. Whatever artistic medium you use, do not concern yourself with artistic merit. The objective is not to produce a product, but to open yourself to God so completely that you are revealing your inmost

thoughts and feelings to God, and God has free access to your inmost parts.

7. Alternate between expressing yourself and being still with what you have expressed.

8. When finished, take time to reflect on your experience and ponder its message. If others are doing this meditation at the same time, take time to share the fruits of your meditation with the group, reverently listening to each other without comment.

9. Conclude with a short prayer or possibly with a hymn.

Here are some art forms you may want to try. It can be fruitful to try something you would not normally select. Sometimes God speaks most powerfully through unfamiliar channels.

• *Draw.* Use coloring pens, with a good selection of colors available. At the very least have red, yellow, blue, green, black, and brown. It is good to have both bold colors and pastels to choose from. Express yourself by the colors you choose and the movement of the pens. What you render may be either abstract or naturalistic.

• *Write.* You may write a stream of consciousness, a story, a poem, a hymn to a familiar tune, a letter to God, or a conversation between objects or characters in the Scripture. Do not worry about punctuation, spelling, grammar, or sentence structure. Try not to censor what you are writing. Just let the words tumble out.

• *Modeling clay.* Use real clay that is firm and can hold its shape, not Plasticine. You may pound, rip it open, or break it into small pieces. Or caress it, gently molding it. Consider using something like a chopstick or knitting needle to puncture or etch the surface. Let the clay speak to you by how it responds. For instance, if the clay is cold and hard when you begin and becomes more malleable from the warmth of your hands, that may say something to you. Clay offers a fluid way of meditating that can take you from one place to another, sometimes ending up in new and surprising territory. As you alternate between working with the clay and being still, let God mold you.

• *Make a collage.* Slowly and contemplatively, go about looking for items that express what you are sensing or feeling. In good weather, things from nature can be especially evocative. When you are finished collecting, meditatively arrange what you have found on construction paper, poster paper, fabric, or a board. As an alternative, you may reflectively look through magazines and picture calendars to find pictures and words that connect with your meditation. Cut them out and develop a collage by mounting images from the printed page on construction paper.

• *Make a mobile.* Wander about, indoors or out, looking for small objects, manufactured or natural, that speak to you as you hold your life situation and your Scripture text in your heart. As an alternative you may leaf through magazines, cutting out pictures and captions to which you gravitate. Mount the pictures on construction paper and, if you want, put them together to create three-dimensional shapes. Find a branch or a kind of hanger, and using clear fishing line, construct a mobile. Ponder balance and relationships as you put it together, letting your thoughts float freely throughout.

• *Create a meditation garden.* Meander around outdoors looking for small things that convey what you are thinking and feeling. Find some moss, if possible. Then, fill a baking or broiling pan or else a sturdy, shallow box with soil. Slowly and reflectively arrange what you have collected to make a garden.

• *Create a rock garden.* Wander around with a bucket or basket, collecting stones that you feel drawn to. Next, fill a flat, shallow container with clean, fine sand that is slightly damp. Slowly and contemplatively select stones from those you have gathered, arranging them in the sand. Keep it simple. An uneven number of clusters and clusters with uneven numbers of stones work best. Consider size, shape, texture, coloration, cracks, crevices, and angles as you slowly make your arrangement. Preserve plenty of open space. Avoid clutter. After the rocks are in place, take a wooden fork or some implement to rake some wavy parallel lines in the sand.

These are only a few of many possibilities that can be used for personal discernment in group settings or by individuals on their own. These same creative meditation activities can be used to address community issues in group retreats. Fully developed meditation exercises may be downloaded from the *Heartlinks* page on the Listening Hearts website, www.listeninghearts.org. Listening Hearts also can help leaders to conduct a wide range of retreats of any length, for either clergy groups or congregations. In-depth leadership training workshops are also available.

SUGGESTED SCRIPTURE
TEXTS FOR MEDITATION

. . . *If I speak in the tongues of mortals and of angels, but do not have love, I am a noisy gong or a clanging cymbal.* (1 Corinthians 13:1b)

Do not be conformed to this world, but be transformed. . . . (Romans 12:2)

Be still before the Lord, and wait patiently. . . . (Psalm 37:7)

Commit your way to the Lord; trust in him, and he will act. (Psalm 37:5)

If you continue in my word . . . you will know the truth . . . (John 8:31–32)

. . . *the word is very near you. It is in your mouth and in your heart, so that you can do it.* (Deuteronomy 30:14, ESV)

I am the vine, you are the branches. Those who abide in me and I in them bear much fruit, because apart from me you can do nothing. (John 15:5)

Whoever serves me must follow me, and where I am, there will my servant be also. . . (John 12:26)

In quietness and trust is your strength. (Isaiah 30:15, NIV)

The word I spoke . . . did not sway you with clever arguments; it carried conviction by spiritual power, so that your faith might be built not on human wisdom but on the power of God. (1 Corinthians 2:4-5, REB)

Unless the Lord builds the house, those who build it labor in vain. (Psalm 127:1)

What you are doing is not good. You will surely wear yourself out . . . you cannot do it alone. (Exodus 18:17)

Appendix 3
The Listening Hearts Clergy Support Group

The guiding principle of a Listening Hearts Clergy Support Group is to be tuned in to God and one another. This provides a firm foundation on which to build strong and supportive relationships. Through deep prayerful listening, members can help each other work through personal problems and resolve professional issues they face in common. By integrating carefully posed questions[1] and imaginative engagement with Scripture into the practice of reverent listening, members of the group become knit together in Christ as they mature in their relationship with God.

The suggested amount of time for a meeting is three and a half hours. Although this may be longer than the norm, the generous allotment of time makes it possible to include four essential elements that help cultivate deep spiritual friendships and intimacy with God: conviviality, using the intellect, engaging the imagination, and serious attention to contemplative prayer. Longer meetings, properly structured, are more fruitful. If time is a problem, it is worth meeting less often in order to schedule longer meetings.

Prior to the first meeting, members need to read *Keeping in Tune with God: Listening Hearts Discernment for Clergy*. The initial meeting can begin with a leisurely meal, during which each member takes a turn to say something about himself or herself, offers some reflections on *Keeping in Tune with God*, and gives some thoughts on the prospect of the Listening Hearts Clergy Support Group. Reserve at least an hour at the end of the meeting to process the Discernment Listening Guidelines, which are briefly listed in Appendix 1. Each person needs a copy. Going around the circle, each person in turn reads aloud one guideline, taking enough time between readers for everyone to assimilate the guideline. During the pause, anyone who wants to offer comments, raise questions, or voice concerns may do so. It is important that the Listening Guidelines not be imposed on the group, but that the group work through any concerns until a common understanding emerges. The guidelines are developed specifically for spiritual discernment and are interdependent, with each one supporting the others. If some people are skeptical even after the group has amply considered them, perhaps they would be willing to use them for a few meetings to let their experience tell them if they are effective.

SUGGESTED FORMAT FOR SUBSEQUENT MEETINGS

Begin promptly at the designated starting time.
1. Start with a meal (breakfast for a morning meeting, lunch for an afternoon meeting) or, at the

very least, substantial refreshments. Use this meal-time as an opportunity for members to bring one another up to date on what has been going on in their lives. In the course of the meal, establish the focus for the discernment segment of the meeting. Perhaps one person is wrestling with a particularly difficult situation, either personal or professional. Or maybe some dilemma is bothering everyone in the group. Make sure that the mealtime does not exceed forty minutes.

2. At the conclusion of the meal, gather in a circle of chairs. Begin with a simple chant or a short prayer. Then fall into a centering silence for ten minutes. Conclude the silence with the timekeeper saying "Amen." Then, take out the Discernment Listening Guidelines and go around the circle, with each person in sequence reading one aloud. Allow a brief pause between readers.

If discerning one person's issue:

1. The person appointed to convene the session invites the person seeking discernment or focus person to clearly and concisely identify the issue, wording it as a question addressed to God (since the group seeks merely to be a channel of God's guidance). After this, the focus person briefly explains the situation. The group does not need to know all the details, but does need to know the precise difficulty, any essential background, the cast of characters, and the major events that have marked the situation as it has developed. This presentation should take about five minutes.

2. Next comes an opportunity for the group to ask questions to make sure everyone grasps the situation and is clear about the question.

3. Now the group falls into a silence out of which members can ask questions to help identify options and evaluate alternatives.

4. Then come reflective questions to help the focus person explore the issue prayerfully.

5. Now the pace slows, with no more informational or reflective questions. The group enters a profound centered silence so that questions come infrequently and from deep within, geared to tapping into the imagination (see Appendix 2 of *Listening Hearts*, the section headed "Discernment Questions").

6. No later that twenty minutes before closing time, the convener invites the focus person to articulate any clarity that has emerged and reflect on the presence or absence of signs of the Spirit (see Chapter Five of both *Listening Hearts* and *Grounded in God*).

7. No later than ten minutes before closing time, consider together whether there is a shared sense of God's peace present. If anyone is churned up inside or uncomfortable about the direction in which the focus person seems to be heading, it is essential for that person to speak up. It may be a sign that it would be beneficial for everyone to continue to hold the situation in prayer and revisit it at a future meeting.

8. Conclude by reading the Thomas Merton Prayer (on the last page of *Listening Hearts*) and passing the Peace.

If the discernment is around a group concern:

Each person will need a Bible.

1. Begin by working together to frame the issue in the form of a question addressed to God. This will help steer the group away from discussion, debate, and problem solving. Do not formulate a multiple-choice question, which sets limits on God's options. The objective is not to get an answer, but to find the flow of the Spirit and enter into it in order to be carried where God would have the group go.

2. Next, share thoughts and feelings that relate to the designated subject. Try to follow the Discernment Listening Guidelines. Everyone should take responsibility for helping the group stay faithful to these guidelines.

3. At least an hour and a half before closing time, become silent. Allow about a half hour for members of the group to silently leaf through the Bible, looking for passages that seem to speak to the issue under consideration and marking the passages.

4. Next, one by one, each person shares the passages they have found: For each passage, state the reference, give others time to find it in their Bibles, read the text aloud, and say something about how it speaks to you.

5. After everyone has had a turn, take time to identify common threads and point out how various passages inform each other.

6. Take some time to sit silently in God's presence.

7. Take note of the signs of the Spirit that may have appeared.

8. Articulate what God seems to be saying to the group. Do the members feel a deep sense of God's peace? If not, it is a sign that more prayer and further discernment are needed.

9. Finally, read the Thomas Merton Prayer. Then conclude by passing the Peace.

If no issue for discernment emerges:

1. Begin with an appropriate excerpt from Scripture, such as ". . . await the Lord's pleasure; be strong, and he shall comfort your heart; wait patiently for the Lord" (Psalm 27:14, BCP).

2. In silence, become immersed in God's presence for a specified period—perhaps twenty minutes, possibly an hour—depending on the inclination of the group.

3. For the remainder of the time, members might select a paragraph or two from this book and quietly share reflections on how it speaks to their own lives and ministries.

4. Conclude by reading the Thomas Merton Prayer and passing the Peace.

Appendix 4
Listening Hearts Program Opportunities

You can read about a foreign country and thereby get an introduction to life in that place and a foundation for understanding its culture. After that, a visit can give you a bit of a feel for that culture. But to assimilate the culture, you have to move there and live among its people for a period of time.

Spiritual discernment runs counter to the culture in which we live. Reading about discernment is an important first step in learning about it. But to internalize the culture of spiritual discernment, you have to spend time in it. Listening Hearts programs offer the opportunity to experience this culture. An hour and a half workshop can get your toes wet. Programs that take several days provide an immersion experience. The ultimate goal is to cultivate a life of discernment.

Because a community of support is important to developing and maintaining the practice of discernment, Listening Hearts programs are offered primarily to communities of faith such as congregations, seeker groups, governing boards, clergy groups, schools, and dioceses/judicatories. Each program is held at a location chosen by and arranged for the sponsoring group.

Retreats and workshops afford a setting and structure for participants to engage in spiritual discernment around their own life situations. Silence, solitude, Scripture, song, creative meditation activities, and communal sharing weave together to draw people closer to God and each other as they gain direction for their lives.

1. *Listening Hearts Retreats* give members of a group an avenue to seek God's guidance about the personal or professional issues they face and brings them together in a way that builds Christian community. These retreats are suitable for congregations, groups of seekers, student groups, diocesan/judicatory gatherings, clergy groups, or conference center programs. Each retreat is custom designed to meet the needs of the specific group.

2. *Grounded in God Retreats* teach decision-making groups how to work through their issues using reverent speaking, prayerful listening, creative engagement with Scripture, and spiritual consensus. Groups that commit to this approach find that controversial issues can draw members closer to God and one another.

3. An *Eight-Day Spiritual Discernment Retreat* provides an immersion experience in both *Listening Hearts* (discernment in community for individual personal discernment) and *Grounded in God* (discernment for group deliberations). This retreat is particularly appropriate for clergy groups.

4. *Opening the Ear of Your Heart* offers spiritual conflict resolution to congregations, judicatories, governing boards, or any other church group in which members are wrestling with a divisive issue.

Training Programs for Trainers take prospective trainers through the program they will be teaching, supplemented by workshops to learn the procedures and mechanics of how to conduct the training.

1. The *Training Week for Trainers* is an intense six-day event, sponsored by a congregation, diocese, or regional division of a denomination. It takes place at a retreat facility selected by the sponsoring group. Registration is limited to eight people who take their spiritual lives seriously, have leadership ability, and are willing to train groups in Listening Hearts discernment. The training prepares leaders to train groups of up to ten in a congregation to serve as a discernment ministry team. This team can lead *Listening Hearts* book discussions, conduct adult forum sessions, offer retreat mornings, serve in discernment groups, and encourage the practice of prayerful listening in the congregation or organization. On occasion, an alternative option is offered for people who want the training, but are unable to get an entire group together. The "Plan Two" Training Weeks for Trainers are seven-day programs for a maximum of six participants at a retreat house in Maryland.

2. *Community Discernment for Call to Ministry* is a program that trains trainers for a diocese/judicatory to go into congregations and train groups to serve as

discernment groups within their congregations. This program provides the opportunity for any member of a congregation who wants to explore a possible call to ministry, whether in the church or in daily life and whether or not it might require ordination, to ask for a discernment group. This *Training of Trainers* program entails two forty-eight-hour retreats, three weeks apart, that begin at 4 p.m. on Thursday and conclude at 4 p.m. on Saturday. All of the program design sheets, information and instruction sheets, feedback forms, and musical accompaniment needed for the work with congregations are made available to the trainers electronically.

For detailed information about any program, contact the Listening Hearts office at listening@verizon.net or (410) 366-1851 or go to www.listeninghearts.org.

Endnotes

FOREWORD

1. The spiritual writer Evelyn Underhill, writing to Archbishop of Canterbury Gordon Lang at the world-wide Lambeth Conference of Anglican bishops in 1930, opened her letter with these words:

   May it please your Grace: I desire very humbly to suggest with bishops assembled at Lambeth that the greatest and most necessary work they could do at the present time for the spiritual renewal of the Church would be to call the clergy as a whole, solemnly and insistently to a greater interiority and cultivation of the personal life of prayer . . . The real failures, difficulties and weaknesses of the Church are spiritual and can only be remedied by spiritual effort and sacrifice . . . and her deepest need is a renewal, first in the clergy and through them in the laity, of the great Christian tradition of the inner life. The Church wants not more consecrated philanthropists, but a disciplined priesthood of theocentric souls who shall be tools and channels of the Spirit of God.

2. 1 Timothy 4:7

Introduction

1. *Listening Hearts: Discerning Call in Community*, p. 23.
2. Ibid., pp. 23, 24.
3. *Grounded in God: Listening Hearts Discernment for Group Deliberations*, p. 7.
4. *Listening Hearts: Discerning Call in Community* draws upon the spiritual classics and experience from a broad range of Christian traditions to explore the interrelating themes of call, discernment, and community. Designed for use in prayer and meditation and as the foundation for group discussion, the book aims to help the church become more a community of support for individuals discerning a call as they wrestle with issues, relationships, priorities, and life-choices. *Grounded in God: Listening Hearts Discernment for Group Deliberations* is addressed to groups within a faith community that are responsible for making decisions for the community. These groups are encouraged to incorporate spiritual discernment into all decision-making and deliberations involving the welfare of the community at large.
5. From the Foreword to the 20th Anniversary edition of *Listening Hearts: Discerning Call in Community* (Harrisburg, PA: Morehouse Publishing, 2011).

Chapter 1. The Demands of Ordained Ministry

1. As Maloney puts it, p. 40, "I rather like the idea of managing things for God and doing things; and so I move from a state of being before God to a condition of nervously doing things. This builds up an ego separated from God—and a person who is autonomous does not pray. That person may build up an

idol of God which is the object of his conversation in prayer. There is a subtle type of pharisaism that uses God as a static object to give me a feeling of a good conscience. . . ."

2. A paraphrase of the opening sentence of the prayer "For Quiet Confidence" from the Book of Common Prayer, p. 832. See also Maloney, p. 18: "The Christian must learn to be utter receptivity, waiting for the Lord to come in His good time and as He wishes to reveal Himself. . . . As the Lord drew His beloved disciples aside and spoke to them about matters that the crowds could not have understood, so He beckons us to come aside and be still." Maloney notes the prideful impatience of those who choose to ignore this advice, p. 35: "Many Christians wish to preach the Word of God before they have sat before the throne of God and listened to the Word. . . ."

3. Peterson, p. 19, deftly captures this hapless state: "Hilary of Tours diagnosed our pastoral busyness as *irreligiosa sollicitudo pro Deo*, a blasphemous anxiety to do God's work for him. I (and most pastors, I believe) become busy for two reasons; both are ignoble. *I am busy because I am vain.* I want to appear important. Significant. What better way than to be busy? . . . *I am busy because I am lazy.* I indolently let others decide what I will do instead of resolutely deciding myself. . . . But if I vainly crowd my day with conspicuous activity or let others fill my day with imperious demands, I don't have time to do my proper work, the work to which I have been called. How can I lead people into the quiet place beside the still waters if I am in perpetual motion?"

4. As identified by Standish, *Humble Leadership*, p. 30: "Confidence is essential, but when we begin to

experience success, confidence eventually turns into pride and arrogance. . . . Success in anything can lead to arrogance." See also Nouwen, p. 56: "Stardom and individual heroism, which are such obvious aspects of our competitive society, are not at all alien to the church. There, too, the dominant image is that of the self-made man or woman who can do it all alone."

5. Lathrop describes the trap posed by unrealistic expectations, p. 5: "Pastors have experience in being expected to be like *shamans* . . . the ancient and powerful religious leaders who have been regarded as able to make liaison between the living community and the surrounding spirits or between the living community and its dead. Pastors sometimes seem to be expected to do the same. . . . Like shamans, pastors can be seen as able to talk to God for us, able to speak wisdom from the spirits to us, able to get our dead to the right place, perhaps even able to get us all out of here to someplace safe. Again, a responsible pastor will want to be careful here. Unbroken, these expectations can lead to massive disappointment for the community, an impossible burden for the pastor, and huge distortions of Christian meaning for us all. The tragic stories of clergy burnout, clergy abuse, and tyrannical clericalism document this disappointment and distortion."

6. Nouwen, pp. 91–92: "The desire to be relevant, the desire for popularity, and the desire for power . . . are not vocations but temptations. . . . [Jesus] asks us to move from a concern for relevance to a life of prayer, from worries about popularity to communal and mutual ministry, and from a leadership built on power to a leadership in which we critically discern where God is leading us and our people."

7. Romans 8:28: "We know that all things work together for good for those who love God, who are called according to his purpose."

Chapter 2. Opening Ourselves to God

1. Merton, *The Road to Joy*, p. 118: "Our real journey in life is interior: it is a matter of growth, deepening, and of an ever greater surrender to the creative action of love and grace in our hearts. Never was it more necessary for us to respond to that action. I pray we may all do so generously." Hammarskjöld, p. 58, remarked famously, "The longest journey is the journey inwards. Of him who has chosen his destiny, Who has started upon his quest for the source of his being."

2. Peterson, pp. 32–33, notes what is at stake here for the intrepid spiritual explorer: "The kingdom of self is heavily defended territory. Post-Eden Adams and Eves are willing to pay their respects to God, but they don't want him invading their turf. Most sin, far from being a mere lapse of morals or a weak will, is an energetically and expensively erected defense against God."

3. See Genesis 32:24–32 for the account of the wrestling match between Jacob and God, for example.

4. The reverse is also true: Openness to God can be what takes us into the desert. See Standish, *Humble Leadership*, pp. 22 and 23: "When we are open to God, we run the risk of traveling through deserts and valleys of shadows. . . . When we close ourselves off to God and follow tried-and-true paths, vision and programs seem much clearer and easier because we follow where others have already trod. . . . [The

alternative] kind of leadership depends on seeking God's path, a path that may not be completely clear to us, and not upon following the safe paths of human convention. . . . God often calls leaders to lead people to promised lands that can't be seen until the very end."

5. See Ephesians 3:20–21: "Now to him who by the power at work within us is able to accomplish abundantly far more than all we can ask or imagine. . . ." Also, the Book of Common Prayer, p. 831, prayer 54, "For those we Love": "Almighty God, we entrust all who are dear to us to your never-failing care and love, for this life and the life to come, knowing that you are doing for them better things than we can desire or pray for; through Jesus Christ our Lord. Amen."

6. Straub, p. 197, describes the seeker's work in this manner: "getting out of the way and doing less, so that a greater presence can flow through us and accomplish more." See also the New Zealand Prayer Book, "Night Prayer," p. 168, which includes this appeal to the Spirit of God: "Living flame, burn into us, cleansing wind, blow through us, fountain of water, well up within us, that we may love and praise in deed and in truth."

7. Writers in the Eastern Orthodox tradition speak of the prayer of loving attention. See Ware, p. 104, "The essential, indispensable element in prayer is attention. Without attention there is no prayer" (Bishop Ignatii). And, p. 183, quoting Theophan the Recluse, "The concentration of attention in the heart—this is the starting point of all true prayer."

8. Nouwen, pp. 42–43, stipulates that contemplation is not just for mystics, but is vital to ministry in the here and now. "If there is any focus that the Christian

leader of the future will need, it is the discipline of dwelling in the presence of the One who keeps asking us, 'Do you love me? Do you love me? Do you love me?' This is the discipline of contemplative prayer. Through contemplative prayer we can keep ourselves from being pulled from one urgent issue to another and from becoming strangers to our own heart and God's heart." Maloney, p. 22, writes, "Prayer of the heart is the unremitting consciousness of God's abiding presence deep within man. It brings about the state of tranquility, the quelling of all inordinate movements and desires, passions and thoughts. The heart, in scriptural language, is the seat of man's life, of all that touches him in the depths of his personality: all his affections, his passions, his desires, the seat of all his knowledge, his thoughts. It is in his 'heart' that man meets God in an I-Thou relationship."

9. See Bloom, p. 110. "Silence is the state in which all the powers of the soul and all the faculties of the body are completely at peace, quiet and recollected, perfectly alert yet free from any turmoil or agitation." He compares silence to a pond with a smooth surface, free of ripples, that reflects the trees and sky perfectly. In the Introduction, p. viii, Bloom speaks of a man who had learned to speak to God without breaking the intimate silence with words. This peasant said that when he sat alone in the church for hours, apparently doing nothing, "I look at him, he looks at me and we are happy together." Openness to God in prayer reflects a willingness to sit in silence and allow God to speak to us, rather than bombarding God with urgent pleas and concerns. God knows what we need before we speak, and we must cease the flow of words in order to hear the still small voice of God

who desires to communicate with his beloved. Søren Kierkegaard described this insight in his *Christian Discourses*, "A man prayed, and at first, he thought that prayer was talking. But he became more and more quiet until in the end he realized that prayer is listening."

10. See Merton, *New Seeds of Contemplation*, pp. 222 and 223, which explains that in meditation, the job of the mind, memory, and imagination is to bring your will into the presence of God. After a few years, you may reach the point where your will spontaneously comes into God's presence, leaving the mind, memory, and imagination unemployed. That is when the subconscious begins to run an annoying movie. The best course to follow is to keep your will directed toward God peacefully with simple desire, ignoring the relatively harmless phantasms of the burlesque. The real danger is that your meditation may become a mental exercise of letter writing, sermons, or making plans around things such as health or money. Also, see John of the Cross, p. 701: "With regard to thoughts or imaginings . . . which occur without being desired or accepted or deliberately adverted to, do not confess them, nor pay attention to them, nor worry about them."

11. In spiritual theology, the heart is at the center of one's being. It is here that a person finds his or her true self. The spiritual heart is the abiding place of God, where one's inner life and outer life meet in perfect harmony. It is the place where the unique personal self comes into perfect relationship with God and all of creation. This heart does not have physical substance, but it is thought of as situated at one's center of gravity, in the pit of the abdomen, the gut. Prayer of the heart is the

prayer of stillness, of resting in God's presence. John of the Cross, p. 583, uses an analogy to illustrate the stillness at the center, saying that a rock embedded in the earth is in the sphere of the center of the earth where it has the power, strength, and inclination to go deeper, toward the deepest center. Once it reaches the deepest center, it no longer has power or inclination toward further movement. He goes on to say that the soul's center is God, where it will know love and enjoy God with all its might.

To the extent that a person is at his or her own center, that person is at God's center. The center is sometimes referred to as the still point (T.S. Eliot, pp. 15 and 16) where thoughts, words, and action are present, filled with energy, but at rest. This point is the circumference that has been drawn into the center, bringing with it all that is, both seen and unseen. When people emerge from contemplation, they carry the still point into their daily lives. It is in time outside of focused periods of such prayer that thoughts, words, and actions unselfconsciously spring forth to radiate God's love and truth into the world. Eckhart, p. 238, writes, "[T]he contemplative person should indeed avoid even the thought of deeds to be done during the period of his contemplation but afterwards he should get busy, for no one can or should engage in contemplation all the time, for active life is to be a respite from contemplation."

Most likely, even advanced mystics are truly centered only briefly and infrequently. But, the more a person engages in contemplative prayer, the more that person hovers near the center. In the fullness of time, when thought bursts forth from this point, it is right-thought; when action bursts forth, it is right-action.

12. The Jesus Prayer is a breathing prayer. The fuller version goes: "Lord Jesus Christ [inhaling], Son of the living God [exhaling], have mercy on me [inhaling], a sinner [exhaling]." It is important that this repeated acknowledgment of oneself as a sinner not convey self-loathing. Properly understood, it can help one stay in touch with the reality that, as human beings, our personal passions and desires often pull us away from our yearning for God's love and truth that brings wholeness and fulfillment. For an imaginary account of a Russian sojourner who experienced transformation through constant repetition of the Jesus Prayer, see *The Way of a Pilgrim*.

13. See Ware, pp. 112–113. Here Theophan the Recluse writes that if one concentrates on it with zeal, the Jesus Prayer "will begin to flow of its own accord like a brook that murmurs in the heart."

14. See Ware, pp. 22 and 23: In the introduction to this anthology, Igumen Chariton writes that prayer of the heart involves body, soul, and spirit. This kind of prayer is of the whole person, with the mind descending into the heart. It is no longer a series of acts but a state of being, that even when immersed in sleep, the perfumes of prayer will breathe in one's heart spontaneously, fulfilling Paul's command to pray without ceasing. On pp. 80 and 81, Theophan the Recluse points out that the first step toward this prayer is the conscious action of praying with the mind in the heart with the desire of being taken to the second degree, in which the Spirit prays in us and which is beyond our power to achieve. We can only desire it, seek it, and receive it. Then on p. 104, Bishop Ignatii expresses the same thought by saying that this prayer must establish itself of its own accord.

15. A little-known breathing prayer is the Holy Spirit Prayer. The basic words are as follows: "Holy Spirit [inhaling] breathe through me [exhaling]." These words, repeated over and over, are incorporated into one's breathing. The unique aspect of this prayer is that words can be substituted for "breathe through me" to adapt the prayer to any given situation. For example, one man who was at a meeting in which people were attacking each other prayed continually, "Holy Spirit, heal through me," and eventually found himself becoming an agent for healing. Endless possibilities exist, such as "Holy Spirit, love through me," "Holy Spirit, speak through me," "Holy Spirit, hear through me," "Holy Spirit, work through me."

16. For a thorough discussion of all aspects of centering prayer, read Keating. For a concise introduction to centering prayer, see Basil Pennington's chapter in Keating, Pennington, and Clarke, pp. 3–11. The minimum prescription for centering prayer is at least once a day for twenty minutes. The optimum commitment is for twice a day, once in the morning and a second time in the late afternoon or early evening. The basic procedure calls for (1) establishing a sacred word to say silently, as needed, in order to draw yourself toward your center at the beginning of the period of prayer, and to use subsequently whenever you find yourself distracted; and (2) sitting in a chair with your eyes closed, head and shoulders upright and your feet on the floor, with your lap empty except for your hands resting gently. If interested in a knowledgeable exploration of the discipline of centering prayer in the context of the Christian contemplative tradition, read Bourgeault's book.

17. Standish, *Humble Leadership*, p. 24, applies this precept to the role of the Christian leader: "[T]he more we lead in a spirit of openness to God, the more God increases our freedom of choice by offering creative alternatives to what we had already been doing. . . . We become more creative, seeing more possibilities. And we are able to help others see these possibilities, too."

CHAPTER 3. THE PARADOX OF HUMILITY

1. Bloom, p. 11, explains humility this way: "Whenever we approach God the contrast that exists between what he is and what we are becomes dreadfully clear. We may not be aware of this as long as we live at a distance from God, so to speak, as long as his presence or his image is dimmed in our thoughts and in our perceptions; but the nearer we come to God, the sharper the contrast appears. It is not the constant thought of their sins, but the vision of the holiness of God that makes the saints aware of their own sinfulness. When we consider ourselves without the fragrant background of God's presence, sins and virtues become small and somewhat irrelevant matters; it is against the background of the divine presence that they stand out in full relief and acquire their depth and tragedy."

2. Bloom, p. 98, reflects on the derivation of the word *humility* as follows: "[Humility] is the attitude of one who is like the soil. Humility comes from the Latin word *humus*, meaning fertile ground. The fertile ground is there, unnoticed, taken for granted, always there to be trodden upon. It is silent, inconspicuous, dark, and yet it is always ready to receive any seed,

ready to give it substance and life. The more lowly,
the more fruitful, because it becomes really fertile
when it accepts all the refuse of the earth. It is so low
that nothing can soil it, abase it, humiliate it; it has
accepted the last place and cannot go any lower."

3. For an insightful look at the distinction between
humility and false humility, see Merton, *New Seeds of
Contemplation*, pp. 188–190. "A humble man is not
disturbed by praise . . . because it belongs to the God
he loves, and in receiving it he keeps nothing for
himself. . . . A man who is not humble cannot accept
praise gracefully . . . he passes it on to God so clum-
sily that he . . . draws attention to himself by his own
awkwardness. . . . One who has not yet learned humility becomes upset and disturbed by praise . . . the
humble man receives praise the way a clean window
takes the light of the sun. The truer and more intense
the light is, the less you see the glass. . . . True humility excludes self-consciousness, but false humility
intensifies our awareness of ourselves to such a point
that we are crippled, and can no longer . . . perform
any action without putting to work a whole complex
mechanism of apologies. . . . A humble man can do
great things . . . because he is no longer concerned
with incidentals, like his own interests and his own
reputation."

What appears to be humility might be pride in
disguise. As explained by Charles Reynolds Brown:
"There is a false self-distrust which denies the worth
of its own talent. It is not humility—it is petty pride,
withholding its simple gifts from the hands of Christ
because they are not more pretentious. There are
men who would endow colleges, they say, if they were
millionaires. They would help in the work of Bible

study if they were as gifted as Henry Drummond. They would strive to lead their associates into the Christian life if they had the gifts of Dwight L. Moody. But they are not ready to give what they have and do what they can and be as it has pleased God to make them, in His service—and that is their condemnation."

4. Vryhof, http://ssje.org/sermons/?p=85, "True humility does not wallow in self-denigration and guilt; nor does it pretend submission to others in order to serve its own purposes. Thomas Merton, the twentieth-century Trappist monk, once wrote, 'Humility is a virtue, not a neurosis.'" Similarly, Martin Buber, interpreting the Hasidic doctrine of humility (Gollancz, p. 354), writes, "[Humility] is never forced, never a self-abasement, self-command, or self-determination. It is as without discord as a child's glance, and as simple as a child's speech."

5. Vryhof, p. 354. "'God does not look on the evil side,' said a Zaddik; 'how do I dare to do so? He who, in his own life, lives according to the mystery of humility, can condemn no one. He who gives judgment upon another man has given it upon himself.'"

6. Mark 10:45: "For the Son of Man came not to be served but to serve, and to give his life a ransom for many."

7. In *Humble Leadership*, Chapter One, Standish makes a convincing case that tremendous creative power springs forth from the humble person who accepts the vulnerability that comes with undefended openness to God.

8. See Vryhof, http://ssje.org/sermons/?p=85. "According to the fourteenth-century Flemish mystic John Ruusbroec, such humility reflects 'an interior bowing of the heart and mind before the transcendent mystery

of God.'" Similarly (Journals 4:184), Merton reflected on how his passionate striving toward a worthy goal was doomed if he failed to humbly acknowledge his total reliance on God: "Yesterday, day of recollection, I realized again above all my need for profound and total humility—especially in relation to any work I may do for peace. Humility is more important than zeal. Descent into nothingness and dependence on God. Otherwise I am just fighting the world with its own weapons and there the world is unbeatable."

9. Hopkins, p. 26. The nineteenth-century mystical poet alludes to this awestruck moment of revelation in the opening lines of his poem, "God's Grandeur": "The world is charged with the grandeur of God. It will flame out, like shining from shook foil. . . ."

10. http://www.albatrus.org/english/potpourri/quotes/ augustine_of_hippo.htm. For St. Augustine, self-emptying is a prerequisite for the inward manifestation of God's grace: "Thou must be emptied of that where-with thou art full, that thou mayest be filled with that whereof thou art empty."

Chapter 4. The Paradox of Detachment

1. Merton, New Seeds of Contemplation, pp. 203–213, offers a thoughtful exploration of detachment. On p. 203, he alludes to the necessity of detachment for sound discernment: "Everything you love for its own sake, outside of God alone, blinds your intellect and destroys your judgment of moral values." And, "When you love and desire things for their own sakes, even though you may understand general moral principles, you do not know how to apply them." Eckhart,

Preface p. x, addresses the centrality of detachment for discerning God's truth, writing, "[T]he price of truth is self-denial in things spiritual, as well as in things material and intellectual." Then, p. 130, he gets at the relationship between detachment and perspective: "[H]eaven is equidistant from earth at all places. Likewise, the soul ought to be equidistant from every earthly thing, so that it is not nearer to one than to the other and behaves the same in love, or suffering, or having, or forbearance. . . . " Eckhart, pp. 82–91, explores detachment using the term "disinterest." On p. 82, he says that God's habitat is purity and unity, which are due to disinterest. On p. 83, he goes on to say that the perfectly disinterested person has no inclination to be above or below, over or under anything, and wants nothing, thus making detachment essential for bringing forth unity.

2. In *Humble Leadership*, Standish, p. 20, considers people's resistance to being detached. "They would rather have the false clarity and certainty that being closed to God provides, rather than the ambiguity and uncertainty that taking new, God-inspired paths can bring."

3. The relationship between humility and detachment is so intertwined that St. Teresa of Avila, in *The Way of Perfection*, p. 38, refers to them as sisters: ". . . still, to detach ourselves from ourselves, and to be against self is a hard thing, for we cling to and are very fond of ourselves. Here true humility comes in, for this virtue and that of detachment always seem to me to go together; they are two sisters who must not be separated; they are not those relations from whom I advise you to part, but rather you should embrace them, love them, and never be seen without them."

4. It is not the information or the idea or the concept that is the problem; it is the attachment to the information, idea, or concept that is the problem. See Johnson, p. 99, "[O]ne does not give up knowledge; one gives up attachment to knowledge."

5. *The Cloud of Unknowing*, p. 26, says that we must keep in mind that the ideas we have of [God] are totally inadequate to contain him, and, p. 60, implores us to focus on loving God with all that we are, and to let go of all concepts of any kind: "[R]eject all clear ideas however pious or delightful. For I tell you this, one loving blind desire for God alone is more valuable in itself, more pleasing to God and to the saints, more beneficial to your own growth, and more helpful to your friends, both living and dead, than anything else you could do."

6. Johnson, *The Inner Eye of Love*, p. 28, refers to the teaching of detachment in Hindu spirituality: "In order to be attentive to the promptings of grace which are the voice of the Spirit one must cultivate what the old authors called purity of intention. This means that, liberated from enslavement to intellectual, emotional, and spiritual self-interest, one seeks God alone. Here again one could quote liberally from Gandhi, who on innumerable occasions spoke about that 'non-attachment' which he saw as the core of the *Bhagavad Gita*. We must act from love; never from desire of success or fear of failure. Nor must we be motivated by anger or hatred or vanity or ambition but only by love, by non-violence, by *ahimsa*." Chinese Taoist spirituality also puts strong emphasis on detachment. See Mitchell, p. 7, "[The Master] is detached from all things; that is why she is one with them. Because she has let go of herself, she is perfectly

fulfilled." Then, p. 12, "He allows things to come and go. His heart is open to the sky." And, p. 22, "If you want to become full, let yourself be empty. If you want to be reborn, let yourself die." And, "If you want to be given everything, give everything up."

7. For thoughts on this, see Mitchell, p. 69, "When two great forces oppose each other, the victory goes to the one who knows how to yield"; and, p. 76, "[T]hus whoever is stiff and inflexible is a disciple of death. Whoever is soft and yielding is a disciple of life. The hard and stiff will be broken. The soft and supple will prevail." And, p. 78, "Nothing in the world is as soft and yielding as water. Yet for dissolv-ing the hard and inflexible, nothing can surpass it. The soft overcomes the hard; the gentle overcomes the rigid. Everyone knows this is true, but few can put it into practice."

8. Eckhart, p. 168, makes the point this way: "Whatever the spirit dwells on, or is attracted to, takes the spirit with it but the person who relies on nothing and is attached to nothing will never be moved, even though heaven should turn upside down." Johnson, p. 159, puts a slightly different slant on it: "If you remain poised at this deep point of recollection, and at the ground of your being, Satan will not be able to disturb you (for he cannot enter those innermost mansions) and you will be open to the directives of the Spirit."

9. For a related thought, see Mitchell, p. 74, "If you realize that all things change, there's nothing you will try to hold on to."

10. Standish, *Humble Leadership*, p. 22, writes of this alternative type of leadership. "When we are open to God, we run the risk of traveling through deserts and valleys of shadows. The vision may not be clear, and

not everyone will follow us. When we close ourselves off to God and follow tried-and-true paths, vision and programs seem much clearer and easier because we follow where others have already trod. . . . [T]his alternative way of leadership depends upon seeking God's path, a path that may not be completely clear to us, and not upon following the safe paths of human convention."

11. de Caussade, Letter VI, p. 197, describes the spiritual gifts that follow from the pursuit of detachment: "Go on then, detaching yourself more and more, and I assure you that in proportion as your detachment becomes more complete you will feel more drawn to God, to prayer, recollection and the practice of every virtue; for, when the heart is empty in this way God fills it, and then one can do everything easily and pleasantly, because all is done out of love, and that, you know, makes all things easy, and sweetens all bitterness."

CHAPTER 5. ENGAGING THE RATIONAL FACULTIES

1. See Ware. In this Orthodox anthology, references to the mind in the heart recur in the writings of various authors.

2. Unless we overtly address our discernment question to God, it is easy to slip into problem solving, forgetting that spiritual discernment is what we desire.

3. Human beings tend to identify options and then choose from among them. If we ask God to choose from the choices we see, we close ourselves off from surprising possibilities that God may have to offer.

4. Ephesians 3:20. "Glory to God whose power, working in us, can do infinitely more than we can ask or imagine . . ." (as quoted in the BCP, p. 102).
5. Matthew 10:16b (KJV)
6. Romans 12:2. "Do not be conformed to this world, but be transformed by the renewing of your minds, so that you discern what is the will of God—what is good and acceptable and perfect."

CHAPTER 6. DRAWING UPON CREATIVITY AND IMAGINATION

1. A passion for something such as Scripture, art, technology, team sports, or bird watching provides a natural place to go for an inspired image or analogy. Yet a given situation may produce a mood that particularly lends itself to an alternate channel of inspiration. For example, what kind of music would most fully express an array of complex feelings that lurk within? Centered silence often reveals a category that can offer a way of passage.
2. An image that arises suddenly, without external control, tends to be strong and indelible. Enter into it fully and without resistance. Quiet, fluid, prolonged reflection ultimately leads to insight, illumination, and an infusion of energy.
3. Through the imagination, we can access what is hidden, buried, unseen, and mute so that it comes to the surface where it can be visible and spoken. When one's imagination is planted in God's presence and reverently encased in silence, it becomes a vital channel for divine revelation.
4. This example demonstrates the importance of alert listening. Had one of the people in the discernment

group not noticed the discernee's recurring reference to an undefined wall, the transformative insight that followed would have gone untapped. Clues are usually strewn throughout a person's story, but typically go unnoticed. One of the secrets of discernment is to look for the clues, notice the metaphors, and observe signs of the Spirit such as energy, joy, and serenity, as well as their opposites, lethargy or agitation.

5. However, not all breakthroughs are heralded by dramatic visual or auditory phenomena. At times, clarity might result from the simple substitution of a word or phrase in the discernment statement or question. Wolff, p. 115, describes a friend's sudden epiphany after a long period in which she was preoccupied with finding God's will. On one hand, she believed that discovering God's will for her life would bring her peace; on the other hand, she was terrified that this discovery might demand a sacrifice from her that she could not accept. Relaxing on her bed one night, she mulled over her problem, wrestling with a phrase that particularly bothered her: "God's will is our salvation." She had looked up the word "salvation" in Scripture and was aware that it meant well-being. Wolff recounts her words describing the onset of her epiphany: "Substituting the words 'God's will is our well-being,' it suddenly dawned on me, in the way that you unexpectedly see where a puzzle fits, that God's will is my well-being. The deepest desire of God, the striving of God is toward my well-being. . . . This came as a shock to me! God wanted my well-being? This was not at all the God I had imagined. At that precise moment I became aware of someone: a presence in time, of space, not seen, not heard, but utterly immanent . . . and in the attitude of a petitioner."

Chapter 7. Coming Together in the Spirit

1. Listening Hearts discernment looks for neither unanimity nor uniformity. Rather, it seeks wholeness, unity, oneness. The Body of Christ is made up of many parts with many functions that bring different perspectives. It is a living, organic entity that needs to function with its parts working in cooperation with one another and tuned into the same mind, which is to say the mind of Christ. That makes for oneness, but not sameness.

2. Listening Hearts Ministries uses the term "spiritual consensus" for what the Quakers call "unity."

3. For more information about signs of the Spirit to look for in spiritual discernment, see Chapter Five of both *Listening Hearts* and *Grounded in God*.

4. While the story of Adam and Eve is an account of the Fall, it also is a story of the emergence of conscience and consciousness.

Chapter 8. Forging Deep Collegiality

1. See Appendix 4 for detailed guidelines for a Listening Hearts Clergy Support Group.

Chapter 9. The Springs of Spiritual Refreshment

1. The mysterious movement and power of these sacred inner currents evoke images from Samuel Taylor Coleridge's epic poem *Kubla Khan*, where "Alph, the sacred river, ran through caverns measureless to man, down to a sunless sea."

2. To learn more about withdrawal and return, see Martin, throughout. Also, see Roberts and Amidon, p. 285, where Robert Lehman writes of reuniting "the secular with the sacred, the inner world of the spirit with the outer world of service," and the "conscious integration of spirit into all aspects of our lives," saying that we can address the larger issues of society only as we free our own inner lives. The theme of withdrawal and return can also be expressed as death and resurrection or journey inward, journey out. The discipline of spiritual discernment requires that we become still to get in touch with God at our center. The test of spiritual discernment is that we bear fruit, having acted upon what we have discerned.

APPENDIX 3. THE LISTENING HEARTS CLERGY SUPPORT GROUP

1. Appendix 2 of *Listening Hearts* offers suggestions for the kinds of questions that help when engaging in spiritual discernment.

Annotated Bibliography

Unless otherwise noted, Scripture quotations are from the New Revised Standard Version Bible. Other versions are indicated throughout the book by the following abbreviations:

ESV: English Standard Version
JB: Jerusalem Bible
KJV: King James Version
NIV: New International Version
REB: Revised English Bible
RSV: Revised Standard Version
TNIV: Today's New International Version

Bloom, Anthony. *Living Prayer*. Springfield, IL: Templegate, Publishers, 1966.

Written by a physician who became an Archbishop in the Russian Orthodox Church, this book imparts profound wisdom about contemplative prayer and establishing an authentic relationship with God.

The Book of Common Prayer. New York: Church Publishing Inc., 1979.

Bourgeault, Cynthia. *Centering Prayer and Inner Awakening*. Cambridge, MA: Cowley, 2004.

This book by an Episcopal priest serves as a reliable guide to the practice of centering prayer, viewed in the context of the wider contemplative tradition.

Brown, Charles Reynolds. *Charles Reynolds Brown Papers, Record Group No. 37, Special Collections*. Compiled by Martha Lund Smalley. New Haven, CT: Yale Divinity School Library, 1977.

de Caussade, Jean Pierre, S.J. *Abandonment to Divine Providence*. Edited by the Rev. J. Ramiere, S.J., from the Tenth Complete French Edition by E.J. Strickland. St. Louis, MO: B. Herder Book Co., 1921.

This eighteenth-century spiritual classic describes how finding God is a matter of total surrender to God's will and illuminates how God may be found in the simplest of daily routines. Books I and II of the original work have now been combined in a new paperback edition.

Eckhart, Meister. *Meister Eckhart*. Translated by Raymond B. Blakney. New York: Harper and Row, 1941.

Meister Eckhart was a medieval Dominican priest who spoke of unity between God and humans that could become so intimate that kneeling, genuflecting, even the Eucharist could become unnecessary. Posthumously, he was condemned as a heretic by the pope. During the past century, he emerged from obscurity to be appreciated for his radical insight. His diligent study of the Bible, strong intellect, and absolute commitment to God brought forth mystical wisdom of great value to people seeking to live in a contemplative relationship with God.

Eliot, T.S. *Four Quartets*. New York: Harcourt Brace Jovanovich, 1971.

In this classic work of poetry, Eliot ponders paradoxes that lurk in spiritual wells deep within us. His graceful way with words yields quotes that can be pondered for years.

Farnham, Suzanne G. *Listening Hearts Retreat Designs and Meditation Exercises with Guidelines for Retreat Leaders and Covenant Groups*. Photographs by Paul Hotvedt. Harrisburg, PA: Morehouse, 1994.

This work puts forth designs for retreats and meditation activities that help participants internalize spiritual insights found in *Listening Hearts* and *Grounded in God*. Instructions for facilitating sessions are included.

Farnham, Suzanne G., *et al*. *Listening Hearts Manual for Discussion Leaders*. Harrisburg, PA: Morehouse, 1993.

This companion piece to *Listening Hearts* provides invaluable guidance for anyone planning to lead discussions on the book.

Farnham, Suzanne G., Joseph P. Gill, R. Taylor McLean, and Susan M. Ward. *Listening Hearts: Discerning Call in Community*. Harrisburg, PA: Morehouse, 1991.

Simple and readable, this work speaks profound truths about call, ministry, community, and discernment. The authors, aided by a large team of research assistants, sifted through spiritual literature to find wisdom on the subject embedded in writings that represent a wide range of traditions including Quaker, Ignatian, Benedictine, Carmelite,

Anglican, Orthodox, Protestant, and Jungian. A prayerfully crafted treatise of nine chapters explores the core principles. Extensive endnotes discuss the complexities beneath the surface of the basic text. An annotated bibliography points readers to the original sources. Appendices of Practical Suggestions provide clearly laid out guidelines to help readers put the concepts found in the chapters into practice.

Farnham, Suzanne G., Joseph P. Gill, R. Taylor McLean, and Susan M. Ward. *Listening Hearts: Discerning Call in Community.* 20th Anniversary Edition. New York: Morehouse Publishing, 2011.

Farnham, Suzanne G. and Louise E. Miller, ed., with illustrations by Megan Murphy. *Listening Hearts Songbook: Hymns of Discernment and Renewal.* Harrisburg, PA: Morehouse Publishing, 1994.

This illustrated hymnbook contains singable songs from a range of Christian traditions. The hymns relate to the themes inherent in discerning call in community. Music of accompaniment can be downloaded from the Listening Hearts website, www. listeninghearts.org.

Farnham, Suzanne G., Stephanie A. Hull, and R. Taylor McLean. *Grounded in God: Listening Hearts Discernment for Group Deliberations.* Harrisburg, PA: Morehouse Publishing, 1999.

This book offers congregations, as well as church-related boards and committees, a way of doing business that draws members into a closer relationship with God and one another. Based on prayerful listening, creative engagement with Scripture, and spiritual consensus, this approach leads to effective decisions that can be embraced by all.

Gollancz, Victor. *A Year of Grace*. London: Gollancz, 1950.

Hammarskjöld, Dag. *Markings*. New York: Vintage Spiritual Classics, 2006.

This posthumously published journal reveals the intense inner life of a public figure who made his reputation as a peacemaker. Many readers will identify with the spiritual struggle reflected in this engaging collection of poems and reflections.

Hotchkiss, Dan. *Ministry and Money: A Guide for Clergy and Their Friends*. Bethesda, MD: Alban, 2002.

John of the Cross. *The Collected Works of John of the Cross*. Translated by Kieran Kavanaugh, O.C.D., and Otilio Rodriguez, O.C.D. Washington, DC: Institute of Carmelite Studies Publications, 1976.

The author, a sixteenth-century Spanish mystic, was co-founder of the Discalced Carmelites. While the ascetic language of this Mystical Doctor of the Church can be difficult for the modern reader, his writings provide keen insight into the interior trials of persons undergoing radical spiritual transformation and offer invaluable counsel.

Johnson, William, editor. *The Cloud of Unknowing* and *The Book of Privy Counseling*. Garden City, NY: Doubleday, 1973.

This book contains two treatises on contemplation by an anonymous fourteenth-century English mystic. The work is meant only for the eyes of readers who are deeply committed to following Christ into the depths of wordless contemplation. It offers profound wisdom for those who have a passionate longing to dwell in God's love.

Johnson, William. *The Inner Eye of Love*. New York: Harper and Row, 1978.

The author, a Jesuit scholar with an intimate knowledge of Buddhism and Zen, here offers a readable and authoritative guide to mysticism.

Keating, Thomas. *Open Mind, Open Heart: The Contemplative Dimension of the Gospel*. New York: Continuum Publishing, 2008.

Written by a Trappist monk who was instrumental in founding the Centering Prayer Movement, this book provides a comprehensive treatment of the practice of centering prayer.

"Seekers of Ultimate Mystery." http://co.convio.net/site/PageServer?pagename=articles_newsletters.

In the June 2010 newsletter of the spiritual network Contemplative Outreach, Thomas Keating discusses the unity that contemplation fosters, suggesting that if the various contemplative traditions of the world could tap into their contemplative dimension together, they would have the potential to find spiritual oneness, with power to unite the entire human family.

Keating, Thomas, OCSO, M. Basil Pennington, OCSO, Thomas E. Clarke, S.J. *Finding Grace at the Center*. Still River, MA: St. Bede Publications, 1978.

A good, concise introduction to centering prayer for the beginner.

Kierkegaard, Søren. *Christian Discourses: The Crisis and a Crisis in the Life of an Actress*. Edited by Howard V. Hong and Edna H. Hong. Princeton, NJ: Princeton University Press, 1997.

Simply written but containing profound spiritual insights, this book describes the foundations and challenges of the Christian life in a surprisingly accessible manner.

Lao-Tzu, *Tao Te Ching*. Translated by Stephen Mitchell. New York: Harper and Row, 1988.

Here is an amazingly readable translation of the *Tao Te Ching* into contemporary English. This book, filled with gems about wisdom in action, is the most extensively translated book in the world after the Bible.

Lathrop, Gordon W. *The Pastor: A Spirituality*. Minneapolis: Fortress, 2006.

Lathrop acknowledges a debt to George Herbert's classic work, *The Country Parson*, and brings a modern perspective, grounded in humility, to the idea that pastors must continually immerse themselves in the sacramental life in order to lead their congregations effectively.

Maloney, George A., S.J. *The Breath of the Mystic*. Denville, NJ: Dimension Books, 1974.

This exploration of Christian mysticism is evocative and grounded in solid scholarship.

Martin, P.W. *Experiment in Depth: A Study of the Work of Jung, Eliot, and Toynbee*. Boston: Routledge & Kegan Paul, 1955.

In this work, Martin explores both the risks and immense value of taking a long journey to one's deep center in search of oneness and unity, which then can unleash creative energy that streams into the outer world to heal divisions. Toynbee views this quest through history, describing it as withdrawal and return. Jung approaches it through depth psychology, developing a process he speaks of as individuation. Eliot retrieves the experience, conveying it through poetry. Martin sees it as an intense and dangerous venture that, if undertaken by creative people over the years, has the potential to bring unity to the world in the fullness of time.

Merton, Thomas. *New Seeds of Contemplation*. New York: New Directions, 1972.

Each of the thirty-nine chapters of this book is a self-contained meditative investigation of a specific topic relevant to contemplative life. The work lays out a feast for anyone who hungers for a quieter, more intimate relationship with God.

Merton, Thomas. *Turning Towards the World: The Journals of Thomas Merton, Vol. 4, 1960–1963 (The Pivotal Years)*. Edited by Victor A Kramer. San Francisco: HarperCollins, 1996.

Merton, Thomas. *The Road to Joy*. Edited by Robert E. Daggy. New York: Farrar, Straus & Giroux, 1989.

A New Zealand Prayer Book/He Karakia Mihinare o Aotearoa. San Francisco: HarperCollins, 1997.

Nouwen, Henri J.M. *In the Name of Jesus: Reflections on Christian Leadership*. New York: Crossroads, 1989.

A highly regarded work by a renowned writer on spiritual matters, this book holds up the practice of prayer and forgiveness, in place of the desire to be powerful, as the foundation of Christian leadership and ministry.

Peterson, Eugene H. *The Contemplative Pastor: Returning to the Art of Spiritual Direction*. Grand Rapids, MI: Eerdmans, 1989.

Included in Peterson's engaging examination of ministry are his reflections on three evocative adjectives— *unbusy*, *subversive*, and *apocalyptic*—which aim to reorient and refresh clergy who have lost touch with their callings.

Philadelphia Yearly Meeting of the Religious Society of Friends. *Faith and Practice*. Philadelphia, PA: Philadelphia Yearly Meeting, 2002.

This book offers a reliable overview of Quaker history, beliefs, practices, polity, and terminology, as well as extracts from Quaker authors.

Roberts, Elizabeth, and Amidon, Elias, editors. *Prayers for a Thousand Years: Blessings and Expressions of Hope for the New Millennium*. New York: HarperOne, 1999.

Standish, Graham N. *Becoming a Blessed Church: Forming a Church of Spiritual Purpose, Presence, and Power*. Herndon, VA: The Alban Institute, 2005.

Drawing on his own experience, a Presbyterian pastor writes about leading a congregation with the intent of cultivating a discerning community of faith.

Humble Leadership: Being Radically Open to God's Guidance and Grace. Herndon, VA: The Alban Institute, 2007.

The first two chapters of this work contain an array of material for pondering the paradox that authoritative power goes to the leader who is truly humble.

Straub, Gail. *The Rhythm of Compassion: Caring for Self, Connecting with Society.* Boston: Journey Editions, 2000.

Teresa of Avila. *Interior Castle.* Translated and edited by E. Allison Peers. Garden City, NY: Doubleday, 1960.

This sixteenth-century Spanish work of mystical theology is based on a vision of a luminous crystal globe, shaped like a castle, with the King of Glory in radiant splendor at the very center. Suddenly total darkness covers the castle. As the author meditates upon this image, she ponders subjects integral to spiritual discernment such as detachment, self-knowledge, suffering, and humility.

The Way of Perfection. Translated by a Discalced Carmelite. London, UK: Baronius Press Ltd., 2008.

Although addressed to nuns of sixteenth-century Spain, this book of teachings on the spiritual life is a cornucopia of maxims and counsels for the serious twenty-first century Christian to contemplate.

Ware, Timothy, editor. *The Art of Prayer: An Orthodox Anthology.* London, UK : Faber & Faber, 1966.

This is an anthology of excerpts from writings of the Eastern Orthodox Church. Bringing wisdom from the Fathers of the Desert, the passages provide hearty food for meditation.

The Way of a Pilgrim. Translated by R.M. French. New York: Seabury Press, 1965.

> Instructive and inspirational, this is an imaginary autobiographical account of a Russian sojourner who walks miles and miles, day in and day out, month after month, saying the Jesus Prayer as it takes on a life of its own.

Wolff, Pierre. *Discernment: The Art of Choosing Well, Based on Ignatian Spirituality*. Ligouri, MO: Ligouri/Triumph, 2003.

The Works of Gerard Manley Hopkins. Ware, Hertfordshire: Wordsworth Editions Ltd., 1994.

heartlinks

an interactive meditation website from Listening Hearts Ministries

The prayerful listening that characterizes Listening Hearts spiritual discernment is now easily accessible to anyone at anytime. From college students exploring their faith to clergy members with an established contemplative practice, a diverse online community of people seeking openness to God's call is finding spiritual nourishment at the meditation website *Heartlinks: http://blog.listeninghearts.org.*

Heartlinks offers visitors a way to bring discernment questions to God through structured meditations, as well as the opportunity to share their reflections with one another. Each meditation features a Scriptural passage along with a creative, contemplative activity.

The meditation library includes:
Create a Symbol
Meditation with a Stone
Mold Clay
Take a Walk
Water Painting
Write a Hymn
A Meditative Collage

Join the growing community of people bringing the practice of spiritual discernment into their living rooms, offices, and backyards. These simple meditations will nurture your spirit, wherever you may be in your journey. Visit *http://blog.listeninghearts.org.*